D1231890

EX LIBRIS
Mary Kay Brewer

FRONTISPIECE

Doorway—Circa 1725

TAZEWELL HALL, WILLIAMSBURG, VA.

COLONIAL INTERIORS

Southern Colonial and Early Federal

SECOND SERIES

by

EDITH TUNIS SALE

author of

INTERIORS OF VIRGINIA HOUSES OF COLONIAL TIMES
MANORS OF VIRGINIA IN COLONIAL TIMES
OLD TIME BELLES AND CAVALIERS
EDITOR OF HISTORIC GARDENS OF VIRGINIA

WITH AN INTRODUCTION BY
J. FREDERICK KELLY

BONANZA BOOKS · NEW YORK

To Three Little Boys—Billy, Allyn and Dabney.
Hoping That One May Be Inspired To Follow
the High Profession of Architecture.

Copyright © MCMXXX
William Helburn, Inc.
New York

Manufactured in the United States of America

This edition published by Bonanza Books,
a division of Crown Publishers, Inc.,
by arrangement with William Helburn Inc.
d e f g h

FOREWORD

ITH the first quarter of the Twentieth Century, an immense wave of interest in things Colonial began to sweep over the country where formerly had been complete indifference and neglect. Architects, having tried a bit of Gothic, some Queen Anne and a great deal of so-called classic architecture, thinking people slowly awoke to the realization that here in America was a chaste and perfect type, a form which belonged peculiarly to the nation and had been wrought by long years of experience and effort; of struggle and of trial.

Half a century ago but little interest was shown in Colonial history, still less in the architecture of that era. The Colonial period—historically, traditionally and architecturally—was considered quite dull and rather vague. Few took the trouble to study it—none, to understand. The dramatic incidents that marked as vital the two hundred years prior to the end of the British Empire in America were almost ignored regardless of the fact that it was during those two centuries that the houses that now command such admiration in Maryland, Virginia and North Carolina were erected.

Born of virtual necessity, Colonial architecture in the South was the outcome of a desire on the part of the Colonists to follow as closely as possible the contemporaneous architecture of the England they had loved and left. These Colonists were students—thinkers—artists. Always, they seemed to strive toward the fulfilment of an ideal. The dwellings that they left radiate the warmth of feeling that inspired them and reflect not only an appreciation of the beautiful brought overseas by their cultivated builders but voice the quiet, dignified and powerful qualities characteristic of the men who made the nation. They display a careful, studied solution of a difficult problem and today may be considered with profit by both professional and amateur.

It has been said that the early craftsmen of the South lacked the fine execution of detail found in New England houses. Sincere investigation will, however, prove that not only is the South a region of original and characteristic modes of building but that its architecture stands true to the memory of the highest Colonial tradition. In the South a knowledge of architecture was an important part of every gentleman's education and the dwellings erected were the natural outcome of the manorial scale of living the planters enjoyed.

Southern houses were not always affairs of great expense given over to master-builders. They were much too personal for that and today these old prototypes are of distinct importance to architecture. They bear witness that their owners were not only persons of wealth but of culture and both within and without show consistent study and individuality. Their lines are honest and sincere, their proportions excellent and their interior detail—bold and yet restrained—is interesting in quality and scale. Their paneling is put together with great care and each carved ornament, every decorative detail shows the practiced hand of workmen who spared neither time nor effort to achieve the best results.

Houses with outstretching wings connected with covered arcades are characteristic of the South—Virginia, in particular. As on the exterior of Virginia dwellings of the Colonial period, symmetry prevails upon the interior. Almost always the walls are clothed with paneling and no home was too small for the formality of a central hall, few too large for cordial hospitality. Some plain—almost forbidding exteriors—display within the walls enchanting examples of carved ornamentation whose rigid scale and refinement are said to be the best in America. In some of the "great houses" the ceilings are of extraordinary height. In smaller buildings they are rather low but in all the proportions are satisfying. The interiors with vigorous, original detail all show dignity and charm and though somewhat unconventional at times, are in every instance well-studied and present examples of woodwork unrestrained in design.

In the South, Colonial designers and craftsmen found many outlets for their talents and here they wrought in both brick and wood to achieve a domestic architecture of beauty, interest and individuality. Unfortunately, in all but isolated instances, the names of those who handled so happily the plumb-line and T-Square have been lost.

As the Colonists of Maryland were much in accord with those of Virginia and like the latter lived on vast plantations, it is but natural that the early architecture of these two states should have much in common. Lives of individual isolation were enjoyed by the most notable men of both colonies. Annapolis and Williamsburg were miniature English towns and their buildings show, probably, the most perfect form of early Colonial architecture. In Maryland one finds, perhaps, the highest ceilings and richest interior embellishment of any Colonial province. Not only are the compositions good, but the delicacy of the intricately carved woodwork is amazing.

In North Carolina, on the other hand, one finds in New Bern a town which is to that state what Salem is to Massachusetts. This, too, is a river town, a little city whose ancient dwellings are none too well-known and whose beauties have never been adequately portrayed. In certain New Bern houses one observes the finest type of old American woodwork and this is hand-hewn and carved from brittle, long leaf, native pine. It has been found difficult to place with accuracy the date of the erection of these North Carolina dwellings of interesting proportions and undeniable charm for even tradition regarding their building is unsatisfactorily indefinite. It is known, however, that James Coor, an English builder, and John Hawks, from the island of Malta, plied the architectural trade in this province in the middle of the eighteenth century. Coor's work is considered more like that of New England than of the South and his name has frequently been compared with that of Samuel McIntyre of Salem.

The interiors of Southern Colonial houses express not only a sincere love for the beautiful—for the arts—but reflect—at times with severity—the limitations of their early builders. Their fine state of preservation after two centuries or more bears testimony to the sincerity of their designers and the quality of the materials used in their construction

For the generous cooperation of the owners of the houses illustrated in this volume, the author would record most hearty appreciation. Sincere thanks are also due Mr. William Lawrence Bottomley, Mr. Bedford Brown, IV, Mr. Fiske Kimball, Mr. Philip Stern, Mr. Kenneth Clark, Mr. Lawrence Kocher, Mr. Russell Whitehead, Mr. T. C. Parker, Mr. L. W. Ballou and Mr. Archie J. Streat for highly valued architectural aid. To The Thomas Jefferson Memorial Foundation, The Metropolitan Museum of Art, Mrs. Richard Duffy, Miss Adelaide Fries, Mr. Swepson Earle and the John Wallace Gillies Studio, grateful acknowledgment is made for assistance in photographic and historical research.

EDITH TUNIS SALE.

INTRODUCTION

CONSIDERING the large amount of Colonial Architecture that exists in this country to-day, it is surprising that such a comparatively small amount has been definitely recorded in book form. This is to be regretted, for not every architect or designer is able to seek out for himself the existing examples of early work which offer so much in the way of suggestion and inspiration to-day.

In presenting Colonial Interiors, Second Series, the author, Edith Tunis Sale, has placed before the profession a remarkable collection of truly excellent examples which well illustrate the early architecture of Maryland, Virginia, and North Carolina.

The architecture of these states is of particular interest, because it displays certain characteristics not found in the Colonial work of New England and the northern states. Notable among these are a greater dignity of scale, a more scholarly conception in the way of design, and a peculiarly tenacious persistence of the characteristics of English Georgian architecture.

This book is a definite and valuable contribution to the all too small group of standard works concerning the early architecture of the thirteen original colonies of the United States. The author has evidently chosen her subject matter with great care, and there is scarcely a plate in the book which does not offer valuable suggestions to the designer. A feature of special value, particularly to those who find interest in the chronological development of our early architecture, is the affixing of a date to each example.

J. FREDERICK KELLY.

LIST OF PLATES

COLONIAL INTERIORS, SECOND SERIES

LIST OF PLATES

LIST OF PLATES

INTERIORS

INTERIORS—DRAWING ROOMS, DINING ROOMS, MUSIC ROOMS

LIST OF PLATES

BEDROOMS

LIST OF PLATES

LIST OF PLATES

MANTELS AND DOORWAYS

DOORWAYS

LIST OF PLATES

PLATE

WINDOWS

DETAILS

Great Hall—Circa 1660

SHIRLEY, CHARLES CITY COUNTY, VA.

(Note Shirley Restored 1700 and 1770)

Entrance Hall—Circa 1660

CLAREMONT MANOR, SURRY COUNTY, VA.

(Note Claremont Manor Restored 1929)

Great Hall—1725

STRATFORD, WESTMORELAND COUNTY, VA.

Entrance Hall—1726

BERKELEY, CHARLES CITY COUNTY, VA.

Great Hall—1726

BRANDON, PRINCE GEORGE COUNTY, VA.

(Note Brandon Restored 1735 and 1770)

Great Hall—1726

BRANDON, PRINCE GEORGE COUNTY, VA.

(Note Brandon Restored 1735 and 1770)

PLATE 6

Hall, Showing Stairs—1740

Hall—1740

YORK HALL, YORKTOWN, VA.

(Note York Hall Restored 1920)

PLATE 7

Entrance Hall—1751

CARTER'S GROVE, JAMES CITY COUNTY, VA.

Upper Hall—1752

KENMORE, FREDERICKSBURG, VA.

Great Hall and Stairway—Circa 1760

PRESTWOULD, MECKLENBURG COUNTY, VA.

Great Hall—1784

MONTICELLO, ALBEMARLE COUNTY, VA.

Hall—Circa 1799

HOMEWOOD, BALTIMORE COUNTY, MD.

Rear Hall—Circa 1799

HOMEWOOD, BALTIMORE COUNTY, MD.

Stair Hall—1634

OLD LYNNHAVEN, PRINCESS ANNE COUNTY, VA.

(Note Old Lynnhaven Restored 1926)

Stairway—1650

SMITH'S FORT, SURRY COUNTY, VA.

Stair Hall—Circa 1650

OLD STONE HOUSE, RICHMOND, VA.

Stair Hall—1660

PAGE HOUSE, WILLIAMSBURG, VA.

PLATE 16

Stair Hall—1668

CLAREMONT MANOR, SURRY COUNTY, VA.

(Note Claremont Manor Restored 1929)

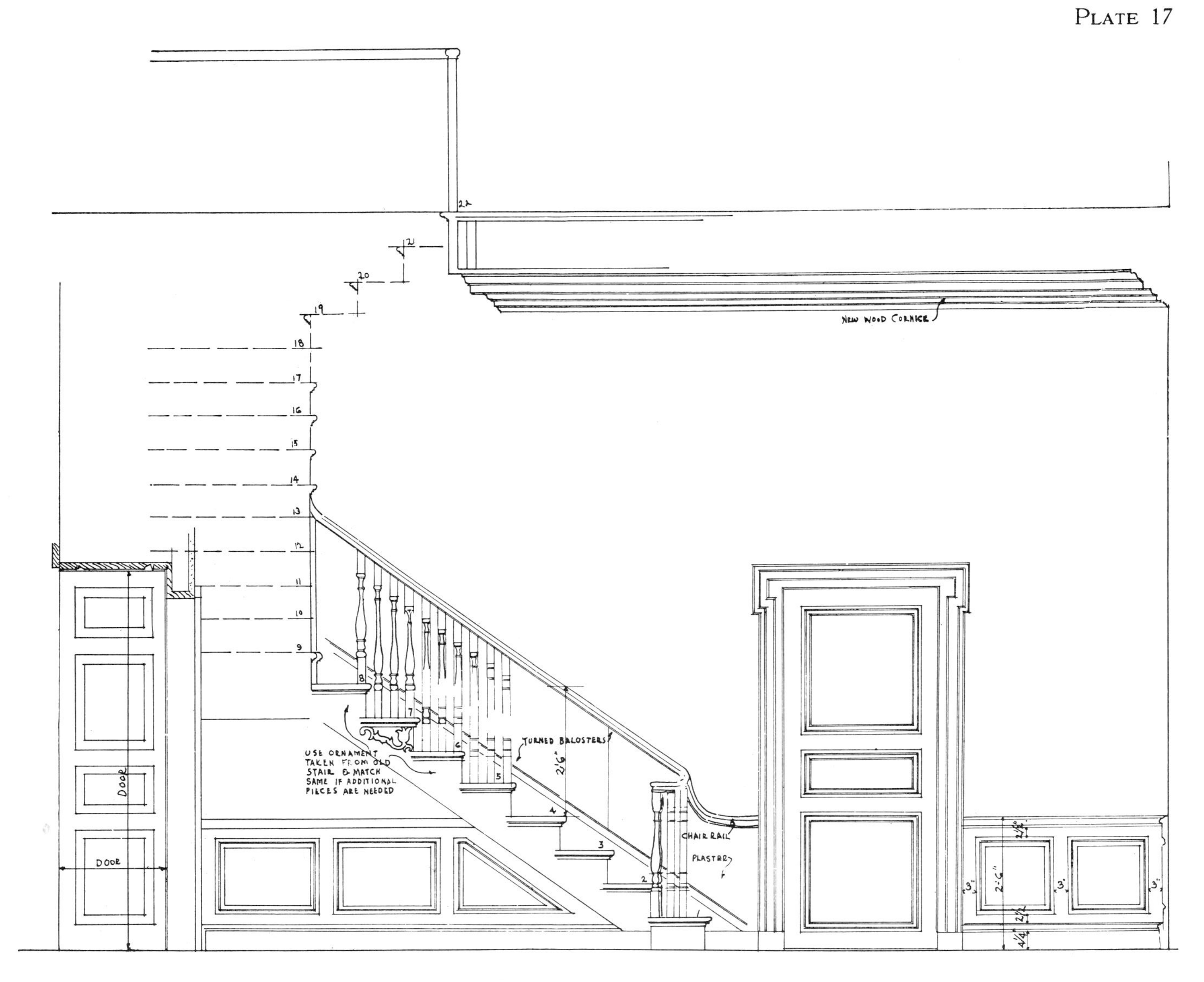
NEW WOOD CORNICE
USE ORNAMENT TAKEN FROM OLD STAIR & MATCH SAME IF ADDITIONAL PIECES ARE NEEDED
TURNED BALUSTERS
CHAIR RAIL
PLASTER
DOOR
DOOR
ELEVATION

Stair Hall, Restored—1929

William Lawrence Bottomley, *Architect*

CLAREMONT MANOR, SURRY COUNTY, VA.

Stair Hall—1709

CHELSEA, KING WILLIAM COUNTY, VA.

Stair Hall—Circa 1710

DIGGES HOUSE, YORKTOWN, VA.

PLATE 20

Stair Hall—1701

(Note Rosegill Restored 1760)

ROSEGILL, MIDDLESEX COUNTY, VA.

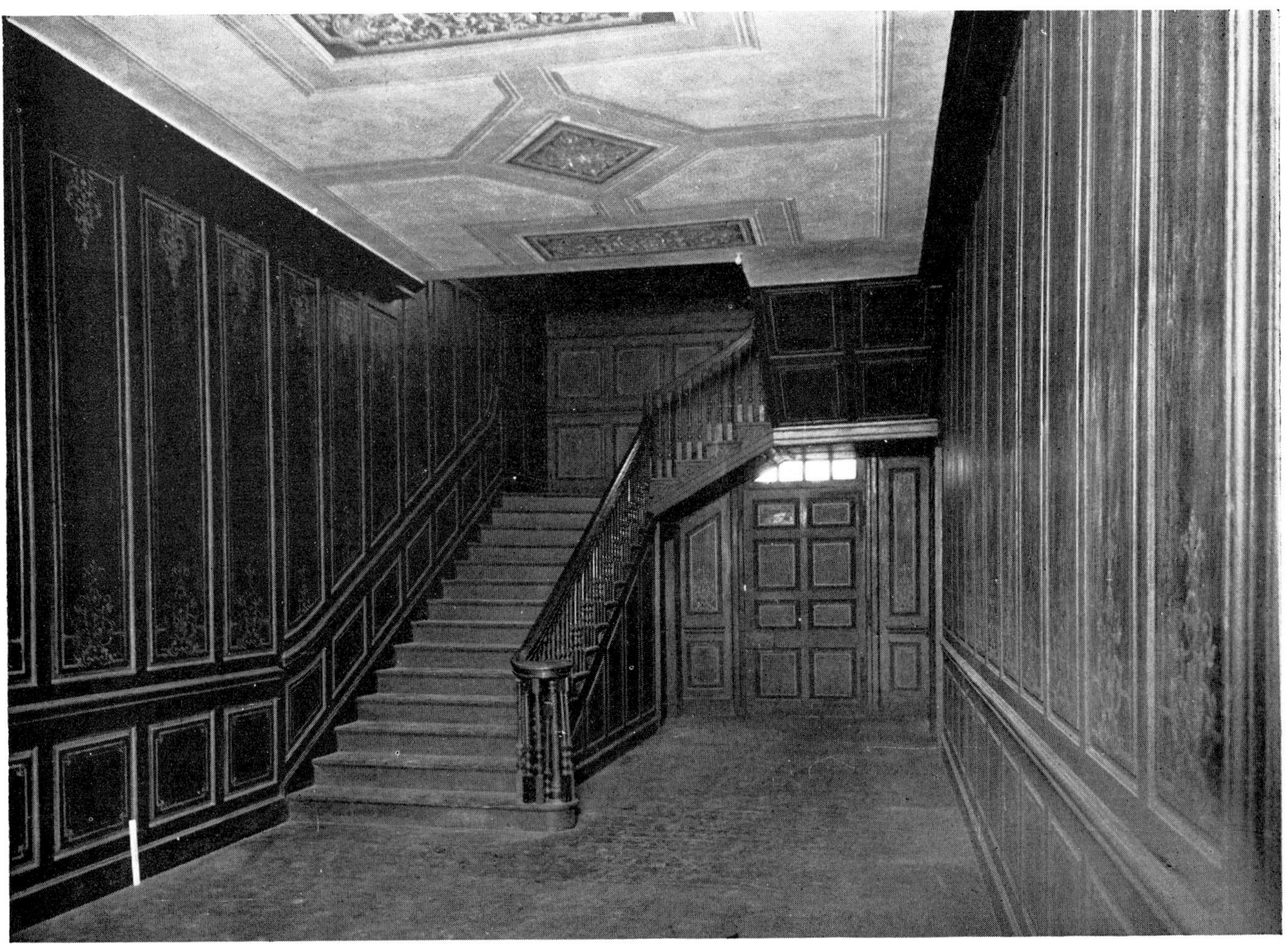

Stair Hall—Circa 1725

WILTON, HENRICO COUNTY, VA.

Stair Hall—1725

STRATFORD, WESTMORELAND COUNTY, VA.

PLATE 22

Stair Hall—Circa 1725

TAZEWELL HALL, WILLIAMSBURG, VA.

South Stair Hall—1725

TUCKAHOE, GOOCHLAND COUNTY, VA.

Stair Hall—Circa 1690

GARRETT HOUSE, WILLIAMSBURG, VA.

(Note Garrett House Restored 1760)

View from Stair Hall—1725

TUCKAHOE, GOOCHLAND COUNTY, VA.

Upper Stair Hall—1726

BERKELEY, CHARLES CITY COUNTY, VA.

PLATE 26

Stair Hall—Circa 1720

MARMION, KING GEORGE COUNTY, VA.

Stair Hall—1732

AMPTHILL, CHESTERFIELD COUNTY, VA.

Stair Hall—1740

YORK HALL, YORKTOWN, VA.

(Note York Hall Restored 1920)

Stair Hall—1751

CARTER'S GROVE, JAMES CITY COUNTY, VA.

(Note Carter's Grove Restored 1929)

Stair Hall—1752

CARLYLE HOUSE, ALEXANDRIA, VA.

Stairs —1752

CARLYLE HOUSE, ALEXANDRIA, VA.

Hall—Circa 1750

PEYTON RANDOLPH HOUSE, WILLIAMSBURG, VA.

JOIN THE
KENMORE ASSOCIATION
INFORMA

Stair Hall—1752

KENMORE, FREDERICKSBURG, VA.

PLATE 32

Stair Hall—Circa 1658

TODDSBURY, GLOUCESTER COUNTY, VA.

Stair Hall—1755

WYTHE HOUSE, WILLIAMSBURG, VA.

(Note Wythe House Restored 1927)

Stair Hall—1755

GUNSTON HALL, FAIRFAX COUNTY, VA.

(Note Gunston Hall Restored 1920)

Stair Hall—1790

SMALLWOOD-JONES HOUSE, NEW BERN, N. C.

Chinese Chippendale Stairs—Circa 1690

GARRETT HOUSE, WILLIAMSBURG, VA.

(Note Garrett House Restored 1760)

Balustrade—1732

BROOKE'S BANK, ESSEX COUNTY, VA.

PLATE 36

JOIN THE
KENMORE ASSOCIATION

Stairway—1752

KENMORE, FREDERICKSBURG, VA.

Stairs—Circa 1700

TEMPLE FARM, YORK COUNTY, VA.

Chinese Chippendale Stairway—1726

BRANDON, PRINCE GEORGE COUNTY, VA.

(Note Brandon Restored 1735 and 1770)

PLATE 38

Musicians' Balcony—1726

Stair Hall—1726

BERKELEY, CHARLES CITY COUNTY, VA.

Stairway—1755

WYTHE HOUSE, WILLIAMSBURG, VA.

(Note Wythe House Restored 1927)

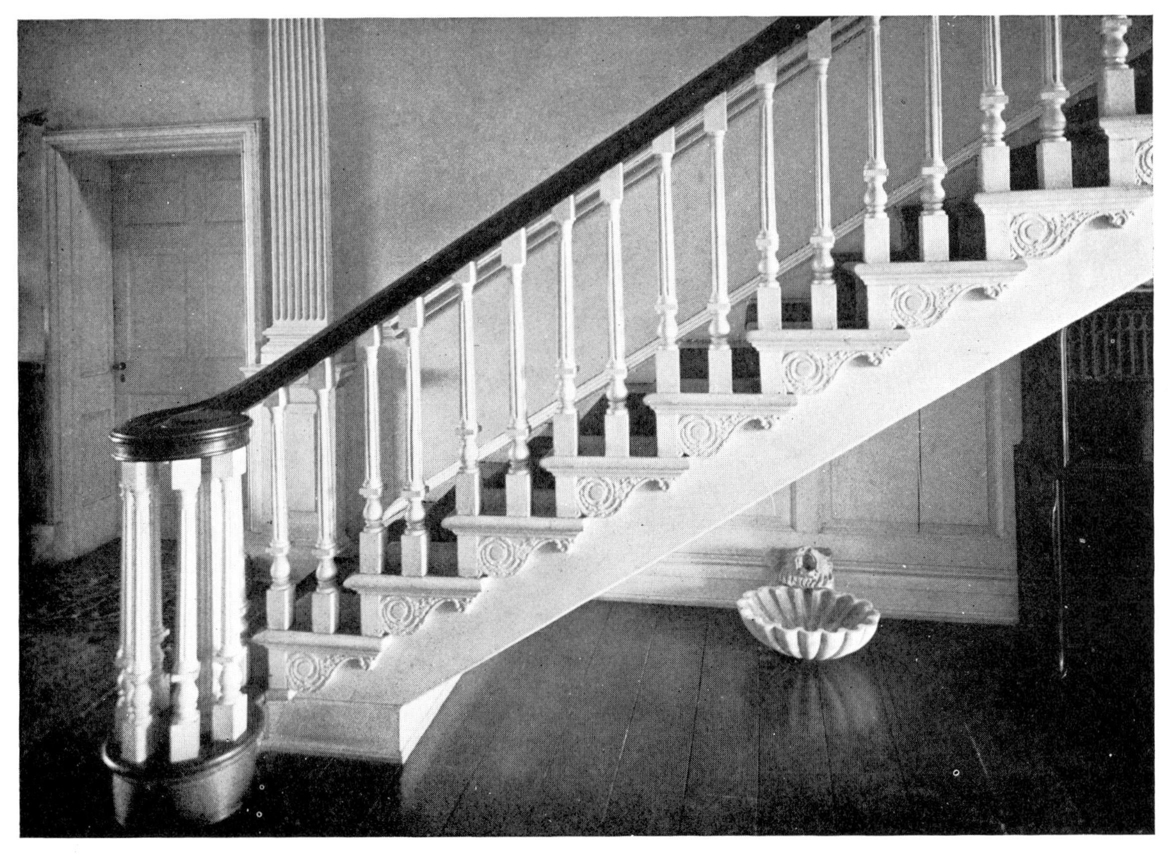

Stairs—1755

GUNSTON HALL, FAIRFAX COUNTY, VA.

(Note Gunston Hall Restored 1920)

Staïrway—1760
BLANDFIELD, ESSEX COUNTY, VA.

Stairway—1725
TUCKAHOE, GOOCHLAND COUNTY, VA.

Stairway—1784
MONTICELLO, ALBEMARLE COUNTY, VA.

Stairway—1770
MENOKIN, RICHMOND COUNTY, VA.

Console Insert—1784
Monticello
Albemarle County, Va.

Balustrade—1668

CLAREMONT MANOR, SURRY COUNTY, VA.

(Note Claremont Manor Restored 1929)

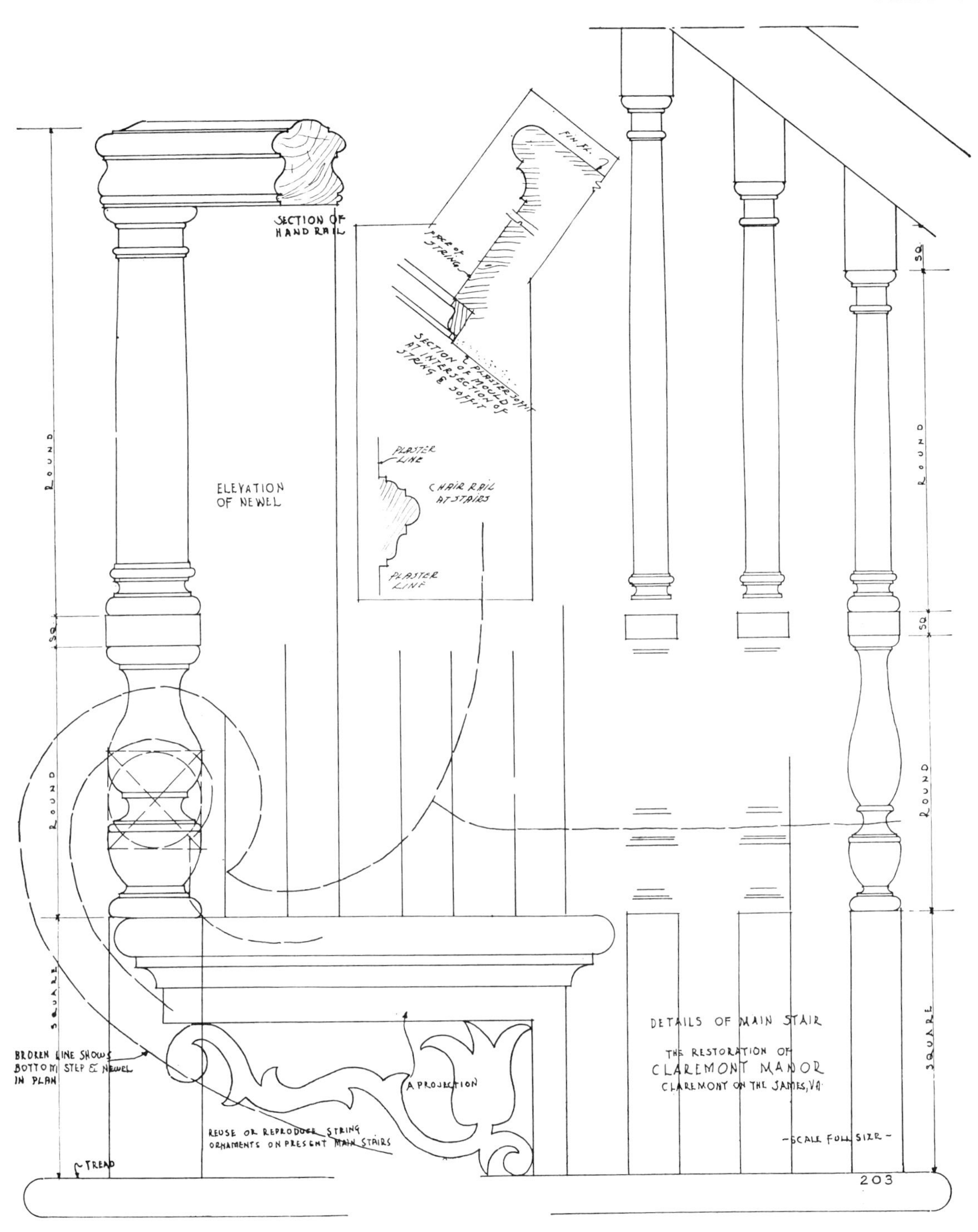
SECTION OF HAND RAIL
FIN. FL.
STRING
SECTION ℄ PLASTER SOFFIT AT INTERSECTION OF MOULD OF STRING & SOFFIT
PLASTER LINE
CHAIR RAIL AT STAIRS
PLASTER LINE
ELEVATION OF NEWEL
ROUND
SQ.
ROUND
SQUARE
SQ.
ROUND
SQ.
ROUND
SQUARE
BROKEN LINE SHOWS BOTTOM STEP & NEWEL IN PLAN
A PROJECTION
REUSE OR REPRODUCE STRING ORNAMENTS ON PRESENT MAIN STAIRS
TREAD
DETAILS OF MAIN STAIR
THE RESTORATION OF
CLAREMONT MANOR
CLAREMONT ON THE JAMES, VA.
- SCALE FULL SIZE -
203

Balustrade Restored—1929 William Lawrence Bottomley, *Architect*

CLAREMONT MANOR, SURRY COUNTY, VA.

PLATE 44

Carved Frieze—Circa 1725

Stair Landing—1725

TUCKAHOE, GOOCHLAND COUNTY, VA.

Balustrade—1725

WILTON, HENRICO COUNTY, VA.

Balustrade—Circa 1726

WESTOVER, CHARLES CITY COUNTY, VA.

PLATE 46

Balustrade—1751

Stair Landing—1751

CARTER'S GROVE, JAMES CITY COUNTY, VA.

(Note Carter's Grove Restored 1929)

Balustrade—1755

WYTHE HOUSE, WILLIAMSBURG, VA.

(Note Wythe House Restored 1927)

Balustrade—1770

MENOKIN, RICHMOND COUNTY, VA.

Balustrade—1790

Stair Landing—1790

SMALLWOOD-JONES HOUSE, NEW BERN, N. C.

Poeana Room—Circa 1650

OLD STONE HOUSE, RICHMOND, VA.

Second Floor Room—Circa 1650

OLD STONE HOUSE, RICHMOND, VA.

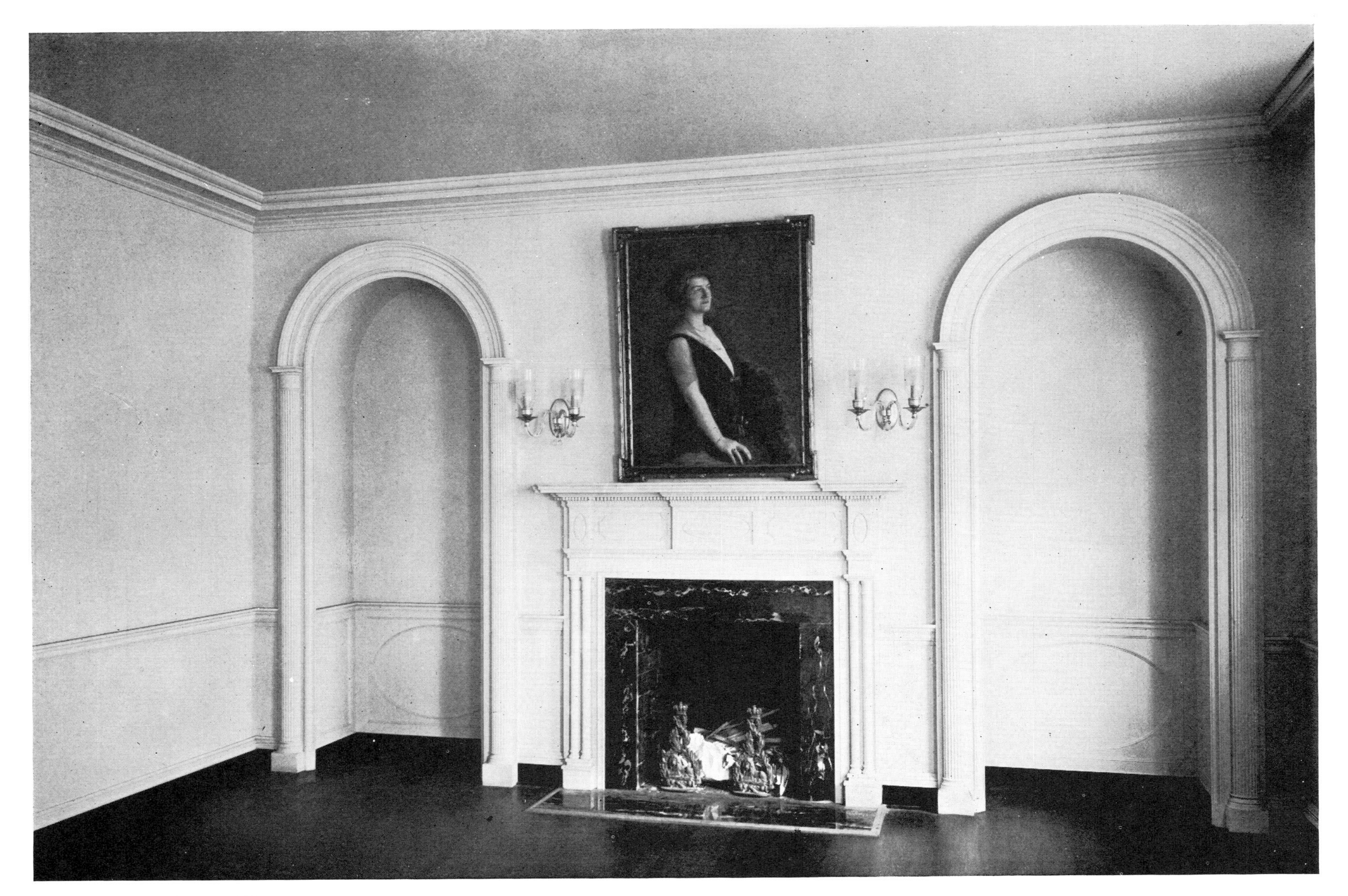

Dining Room—Circa 1668

CLAREMONT MANOR, SURRY COUNTY, VA.

(Note Claremont Manor Restored 1929)

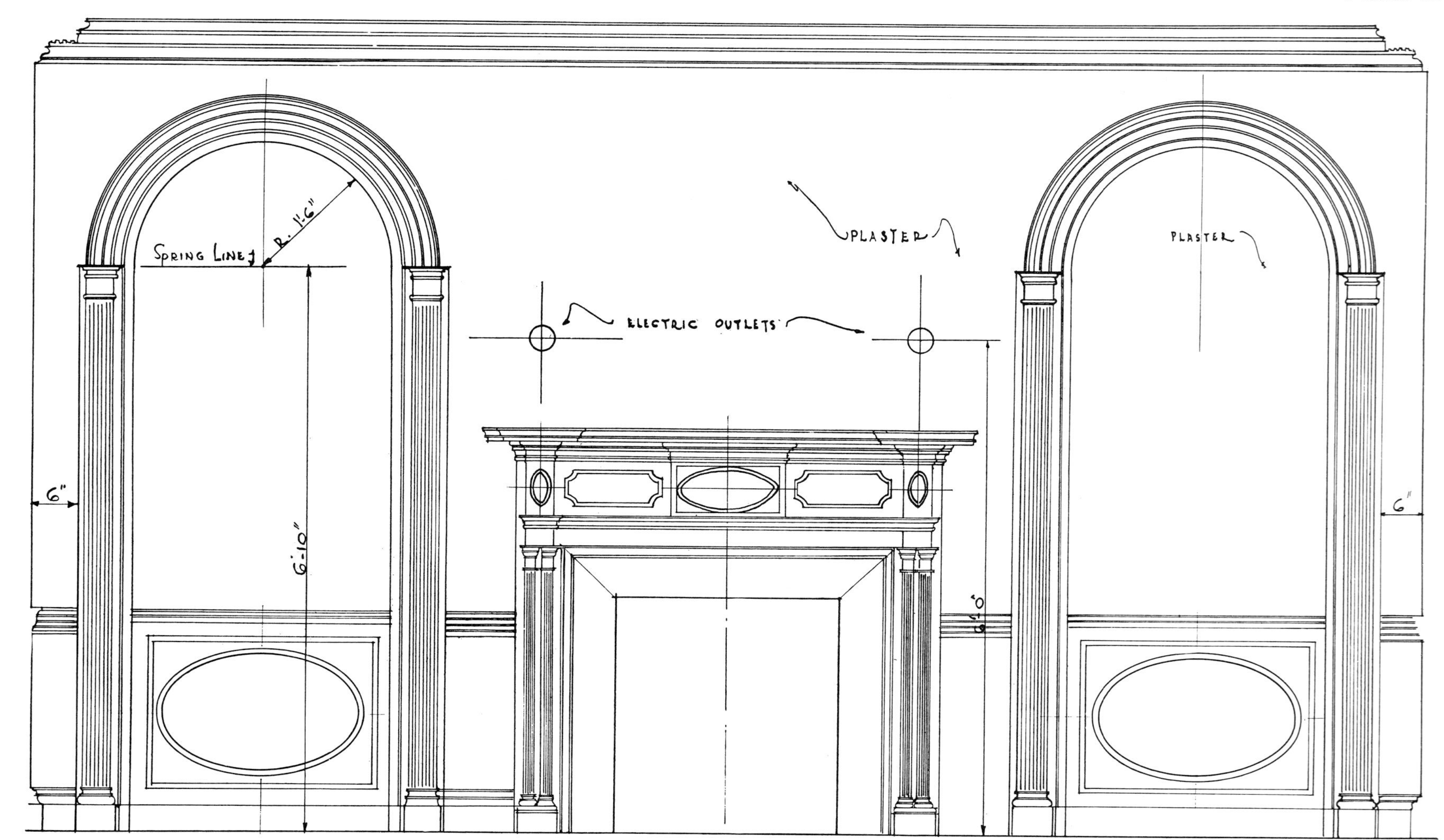
SPRING LINE
R. 1'-6"
6"
6'-10"
ELECTRIC OUTLETS
PLASTER
PLASTER
6'-0"
6"
-SOUTH ELEVATION-

Dining Room, Restored—1929

William Lawrence Bottomley, *Architect*

CLAREMONT MANOR, SURRY COUNTY, VA.

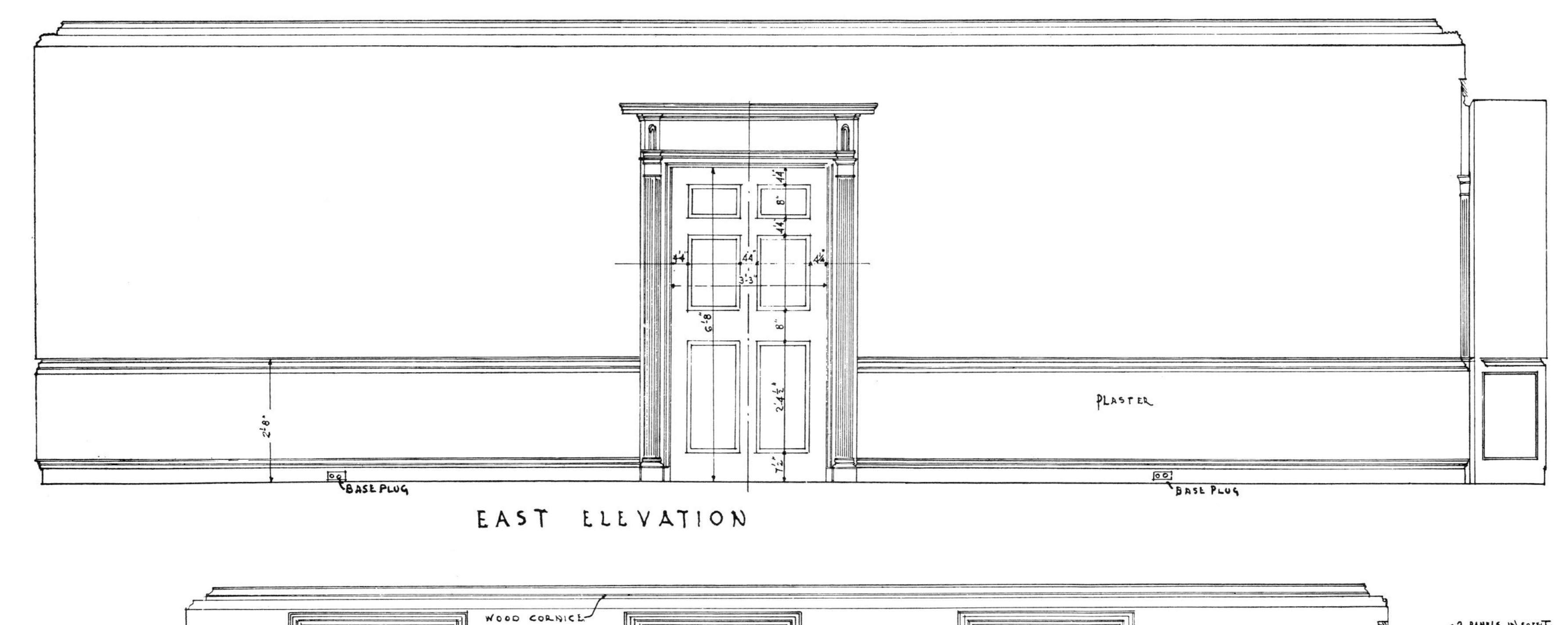
PLASTER
BASE PLUG
BASE PLUG
EAST ELEVATION

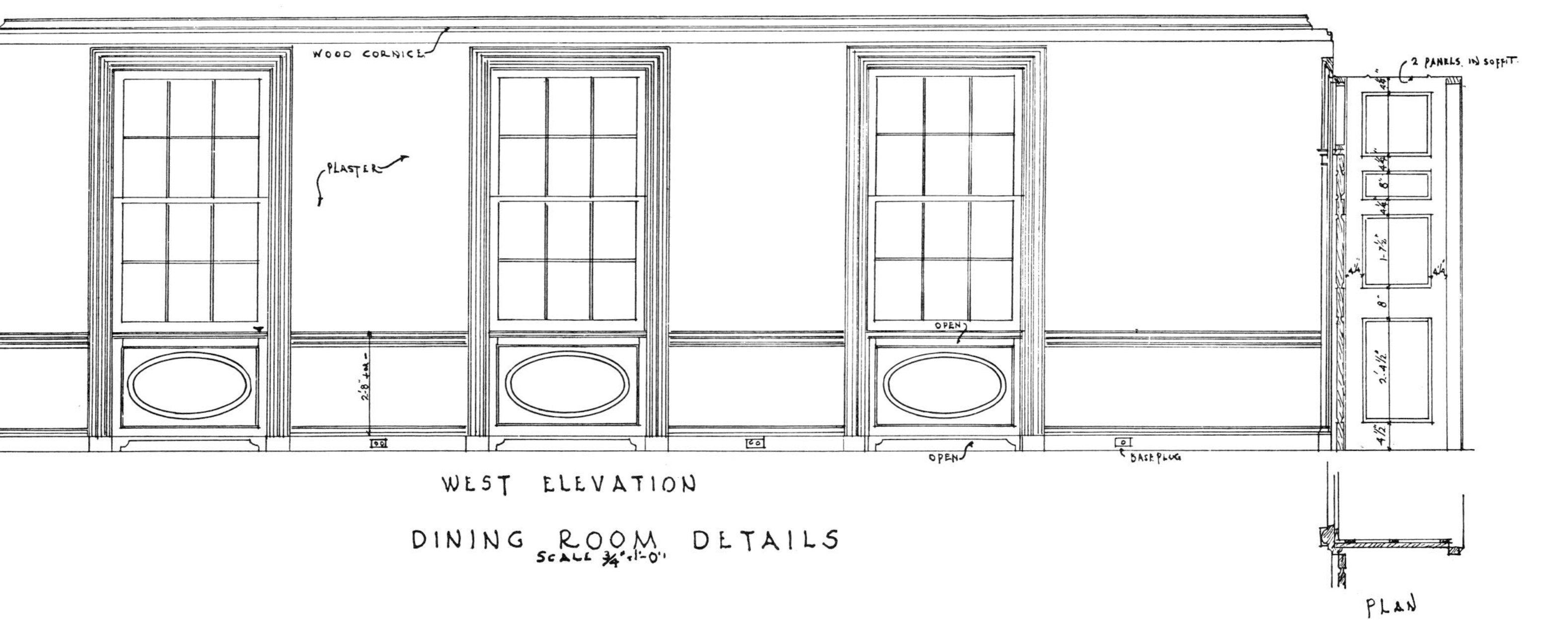
WOOD CORNICE
PLASTER
PLASTER LINE
OPEN
OPEN
BASE PLUG
2 PANELS IN SOFFIT
WEST ELEVATION
DINING ROOM DETAILS
SCALE 3/4"=1'-0"
PLAN

Dining Room—as restored 1929

CLAREMONT MANOR, SURRY COUNTY, VA.

Library—1668

CLAREMONT MANOR, SURRY COUNTY, VA.

(Note Claremont Manor Restored 1929)

WALNUT
APPROX PRESENT HEAD
3
10
17
16
ADJUSTABLE PINE SHELVES
PRESENT PLASTER LINE
PRESENT DOOR
WALNUT
PINE
WALNUT
NEW DOOR & PANELED JAMBS
15
CURTAIN POCKET
RADIATOR
PINE PANEL
CURTAIN POCKET
WALNUT
PINE
POCKET
RADIATOR
POCKET
ADJUSTABLE SHELF
OPEN
WALNUT BASE
OPEN

NORTH ELEVATION (SOUTH ELEVATION SIMILAR-REVERSE)

Library—as restored 1929

William Lawrence Bottomley, *Architect*

CLAREMONT MANOR, SURRY COUNTY, VA.

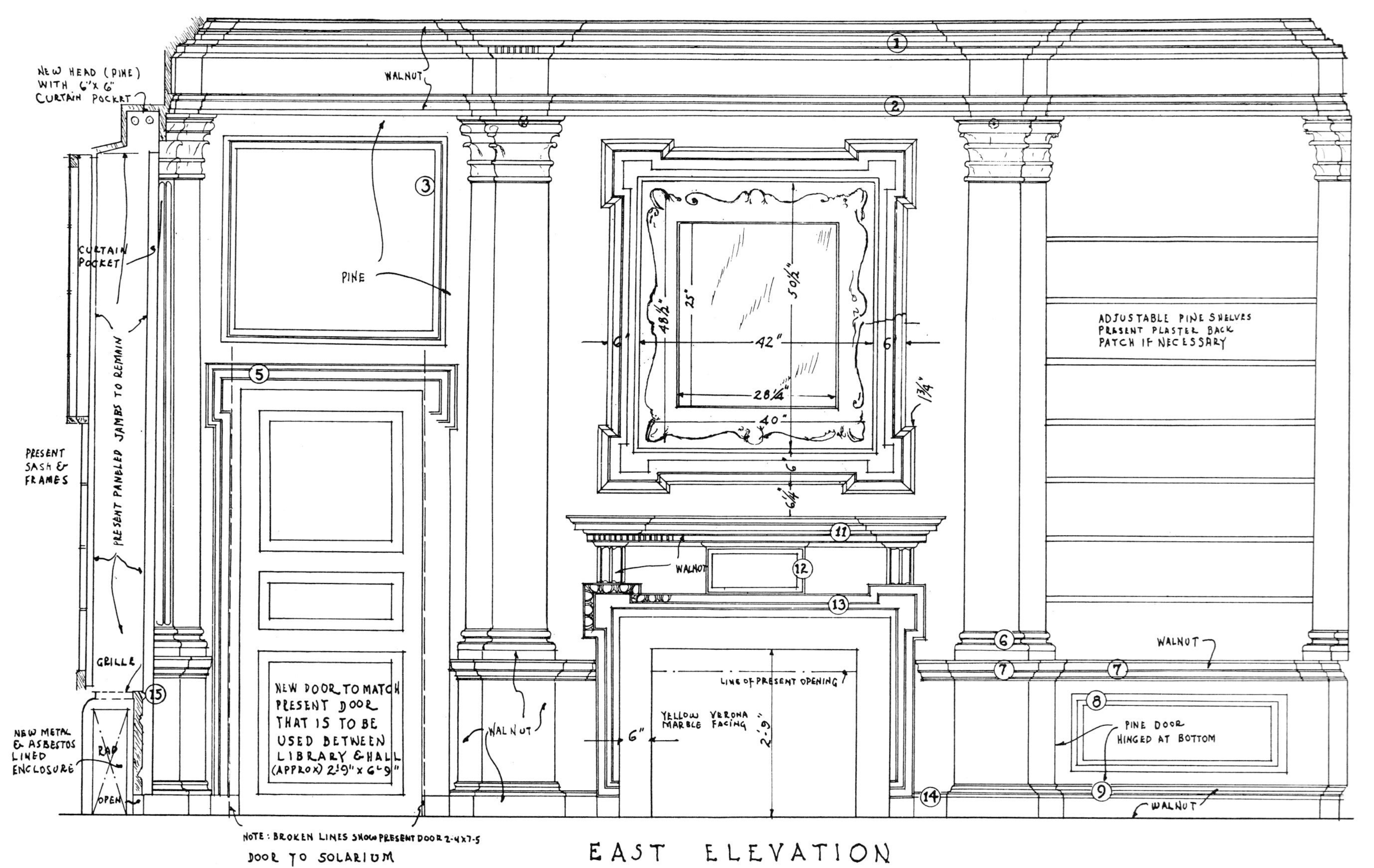
NEW HEAD (PINE) WITH 6"x 6" CURTAIN POCKET
WALNUT
CURTAIN POCKET
PINE
PRESENT PANELED JAMBS TO REMAIN
PRESENT SASH & FRAMES
GRILLE
NEW METAL & ASBESTOS LINED ENCLOSURE
RAD
OPEN
NEW DOOR TO MATCH PRESENT DOOR THAT IS TO BE USED BETWEEN LIBRARY & HALL (APPROX) 2'9" x 6'9"
NOTE: BROKEN LINES SHOW PRESENT DOOR 2-4x7-5
DOOR TO SOLARIUM
WALNUT
48½"
25"
50½"
42"
28¼"
40"
6"
6¼"
1¾"
LINE OF PRESENT OPENING
YELLOW VERONA MARBLE FACING
2'-9"
ADJUSTABLE PINE SHELVES PRESENT PLASTER BACK PATCH IF NECESSARY
PINE DOOR HINGED AT BOTTOM
EAST ELEVATION

Library—as restored 1929

William Lawrence Bottomley, *Architect*

CLAREMONT MANOR, SURRY COUNTY, VA.

Tap Room—1668

The Floor and Ceiling are notable examples

CLAREMONT MANOR, SURRY COUNTY, VA.

(Note Claremont Manor Restored 1929)

Drawing Room—1634

OLD LYNNHAVEN, PRINCESS ANNE COUNTY, VA.

(Note Old Lynnhaven Restored 1926)

The Physic Room—1677

GALT HOUSE, WILLIAMSBURG, VA.

Living Room—Circa 1710

DIGGES HOUSE, YORKTOWN, VA.

Burnt Room, East End—1725

TUCKAHOE, GOOCHLAND COUNTY, VA.

Chinese Chippendale Room—1755

GUNSTON HALL, FAIRFAX COUNTY, VA.

(Note Gunston Hall Restored 1920)

Masonic Lodge Room—Circa 1790

NEW BERN, N. C.

Ball Room—Circa 1793

METROPOLITAN MUSEUM OF ART, NEW YORK

GADSBY'S TAVERN, ALEXANDRIA, VA.

State Room—Circa 1799

HOMEWOOD, BALTIMORE COUNTY, MD.

State Room—Circa 1799

HOMEWOOD, BALTIMORE COUNTY, MD.

Dining Room—1650

SHIRLEY, CHARLES CITY COUNTY, VA.

(Note Shirley Restored 1700 and 1770)

Drawing Room—1650

SHIRLEY, CHARLES CITY COUNTY, VA.

(Note Shirley Restored 1700 and 1770)

Drawing Room—1677

GALT HOUSE, WILLIAMSBURG, VA.

Dining Room—Circa 1658

TODDSBURY, GLOUCESTER COUNTY, VA.

Music Room—1668

CLAREMONT MANOR, SURRY COUNTY, VA.

(Note Claremont Manor Restored 1929)

Music Room—1668

CLAREMONT MANOR, SURRY COUNTY, VA.

(Note Claremont Manor Restored 1929)

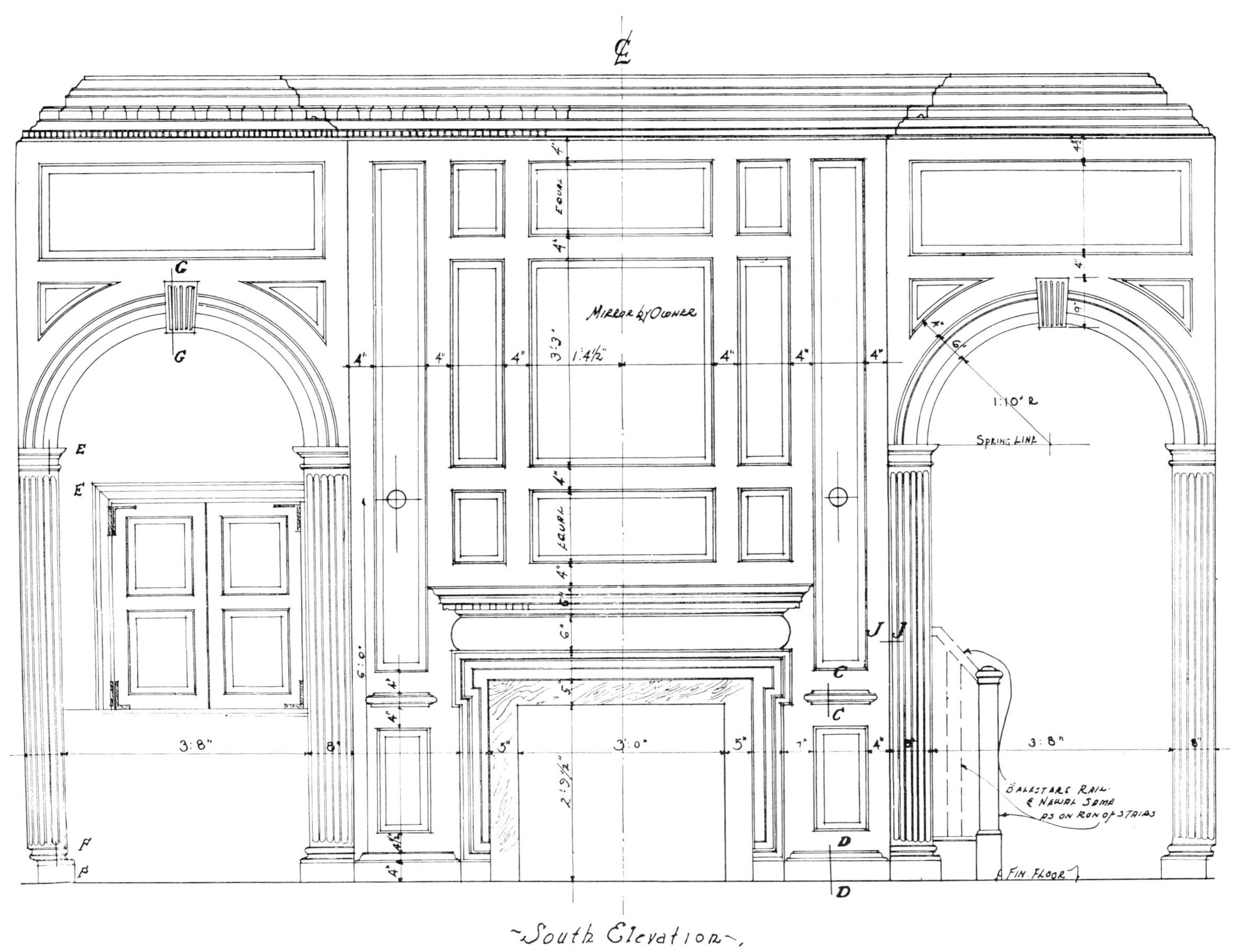
Mirror by Owner
Spring Line
Balusters Rail & Newel Same as on Run of Stairs
Fin. Floor
~South Elevation~

Music Room—restored 1929

William Lawrence Bottomley, *Architect*

CLAREMONT MANOR, SURRY COUNTY, VA.

Drawing Room—1709

CHELSEA, KING WILLIAM COUNTY, VA.

Dining Room—Circa 1710

DIGGES HOUSE, YORKTOWN, VA.

Drawing Room—Circa 1720

METROPOLITAN MUSEUM OF ART, NEW YORK

MARMION, KING GEORGE COUNTY, VA.

Painted Walls—Circa 1720

METROPOLITAN MUSEUM OF ART, NEW YORK

MARMION, KING GEORGE COUNTY, VA.

Painted Paneled Room—Circa 1720

METROPOLITAN MUSEUM OF ART, NEW YORK

MARMION, KING GEORGE COUNTY, VA.

Wall Treatment and Mantel—Circa 1720

METROPOLITAN MUSEUM OF ART, NEW YORK

MARMION, KING GEORGE COUNTY, VA.

Dining Room—Circa 1720

MARMION, KING GEORGE COUNTY, VA.

Drawing Room—Circa 1725

TAZEWELL HALL, WILLIAMSBURG, VA.

Dining Room—Circa 1726

(Note Brandon Restored 1735 and 1770)

BRANDON, PRINCE GEORGE COUNTY, VA.

Dining Room—1701

ROSEGILL, MIDDLESEX COUNTY, VA.

(Note Rosegill Restored 1760)

Drawing Room—1726-1770

BRANDON, PRINCE GEORGE COUNTY, VA.

(Note Brandon Restored 1735-1770)

Dining Room—Circa 1730

PEACHY HOUSE, WILLIAMSBURG, VA.

Dining Room—Circa 1730

PEACHY HOUSE, WILLIAMSBURG, VA.

Dining Room—1740

YORK HALL, YORKTOWN, VA.

(Note York Hall Restored 1920)

Drawing Room—Circa 1750

ALMODINGTON, SOMERSET COUNTY, MD.

Drawing Room—1752

KENMORE, FREDERICKSBURG, VA.

Dining Room—1752

KENMORE, FREDERICKSBURG, VA.

Drawing Room—1755

GUNSTON HALL, FAIRFAX COUNTY, VA.

(Note Gunston Hall Restored 1920)

Music Room—1755

GUNSTON HALL, FAIRFAX COUNTY, VA.

(Note Gunston Hall Restored 1920)

Drawing Room—Circa 1769

PRESTWOULD, MECKLENBURG COUNTY, VA.

Drawing Room—Circa 1760

Dining Room—Circa 1760

PRESTWOULD, MECKLENBURG COUNTY, VA.

PLATE 92

Drawing Room, South Wall—Circa 1774

Great Hall—1774

ELMWOOD, ESSEX COUNTY, VA.

Drawing Room—Circa 1798

MOORE HOUSE, PETERSBURG, VA.

PLATE 94

Drawing Room—Circa 1799

Drawing Room—Circa 1799

HOMEWOOD, BALTIMORE COUNTY, MD.

Dining Room—Circa 1799

HOMEWOOD, BALTIMORE COUNTY, MD.

Dining Room—Circa 1799

HOMEWOOD, BALTIMORE COUNTY, MD.

Music Room—Circa 1799

HOMEWOOD, BALTIMORE COUNTY, MD.

Music Room—Circa 1799

HOMEWOOD, BALTIMORE COUNTY, MD.

Baltimore Dining Room—Circa 1810

METROPOLITAN MUSEUM OF ART, NEW YORK

PLATE 100

Master's Bed Room—1660

PAGE HOUSE, WILLIAMSBURG, VA.

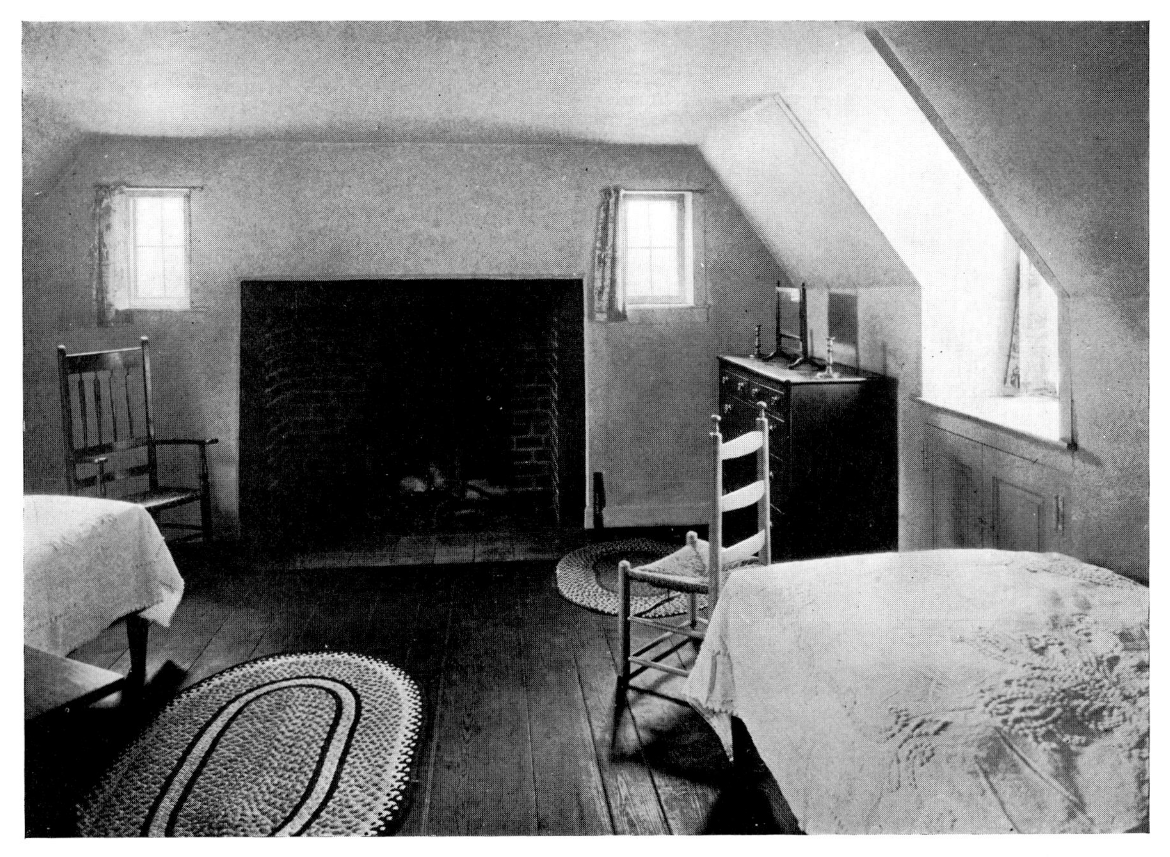

Master's Bed Room—1634

OLD LYNNHAVEN, PRINCESS ANNE COUNTY, VA.

(Note Old Lynnhaven Restored 1926)

Master's Bed Room—Circa 1668

CLAREMONT MANOR, SURRY COUNTY, VA.

(Note Claremont Manor Restored 1929)

Bed Room—Circa 1668

CLAREMONT MANOR, SURRY COUNTY, VA.

(Note Claremont Manor Restored 1929)

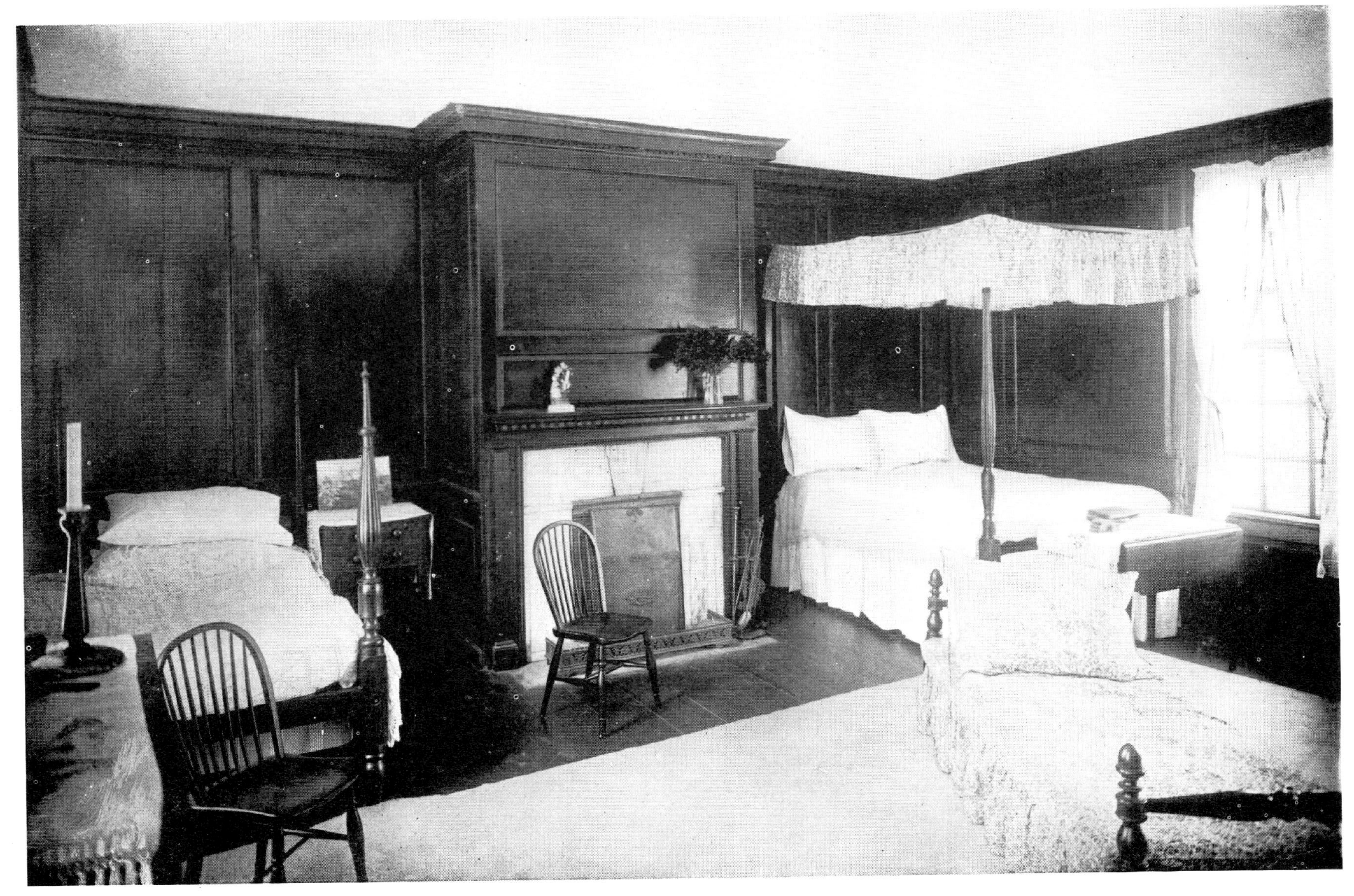

Bed Room—1725

TUCKAHOE, GOOCHLAND COUNTY, VA.

Lafayette Room—Circa 1730

PEACHY HOUSE, WILLIAMSBURG, VA.

Bed Room—1752

CARLYLE HOUSE, ALEXANDRIA, VA.

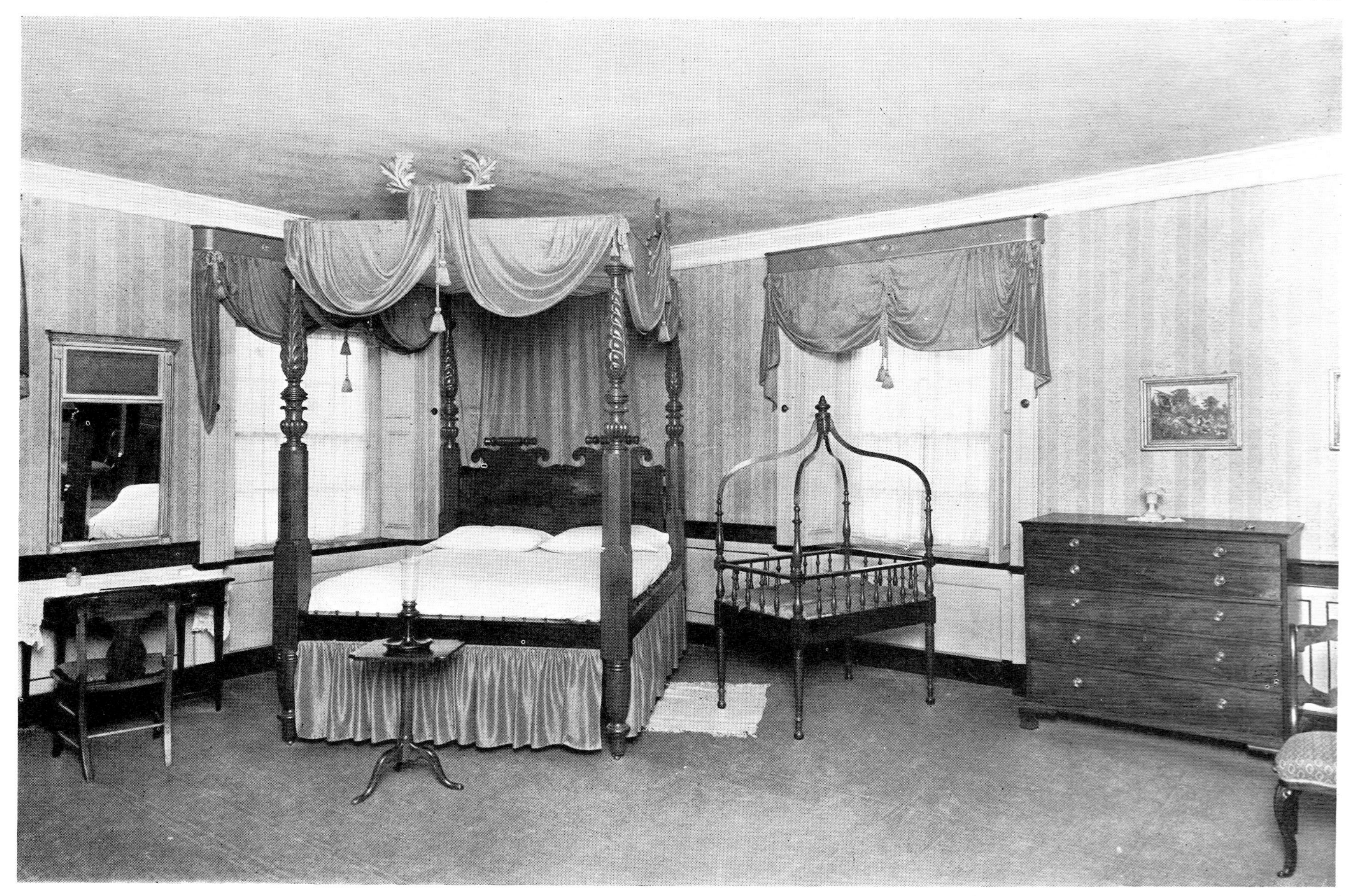

Lady Jean Skipwith's Room—Circa 1760

PRESTWOULD, MECKLENBURG COUNTY, VA.

Bed Room—1740

YORK HALL, YORKTOWN, VA.

(Note York Hall Restored 1920)

Dressing Room—Circa 1799

HOMEWOOD, BALTIMORE COUNTY, MD.

Master's Bed Room—Circa 1799

HOMEWOOD, BALTIMORE COUNTY, MD.

Child's Bed Room—Circa 1799

Bed Room—Circa 1799

HOMEWOOD, BALTIMORE COUNTY, MD.

ONE FOOT

Original Kitchen—1634

OLD LYNNHAVEN, PRINCESS ANNE COUNTY, VA.

(Note Old Lynnhaven Restored 1926)

Kitchen Fireplace—1701

ROSEGILL, MIDDLESEX COUNTY, VA.

(Note Rosegill Restored 1760)

Kitchen Fireplace—1726

BRANDON, PRINCE GEORGE COUNTY, VA.

(Note Brandon Restored 1735 and 1770)

PLATE 112

Original Kitchen—1725

TUCKAHOE, GOOCHLAND COUNTY, VA.

Mantel—1725

STRATFORD, WESTMORELAND COUNTY, VA.

Original Kitchen—Circa 1726

WESTOVER, CHARLES CITY COUNTY, VA.

PLATE 114

Paneled Chimney End—Circa 1700

RITCHIE HOUSE, TAPPAHANNOCK, VA.

Chimney Breast—1701

ROSEGILL, MIDDLESEX COUNTY, VA.

(Note Rosegill Restored 1760)

Chimney Breast—Circa 1720

MARMION, KING GEORGE COUNTY, VA.

Chimney Breast—1725

WILTON, HENRICO COUNTY, VA.

Chimney Breast—1725

TUCKAHOE, GOOCHLAND COUNTY, VA.

Paneled Chimney End—Circa 1650

ROLFE HOUSE, SURRY COUNTY, VA.

THE ROLFE HOUSE IS CALLED THE OLDEST HOUSE IN AMERICA

Paneled Chimney End—Circa 1732

AMPTHILL, CHESTERFIELD COUNTY, VA.

PLATE 118

Chimney Breast and Paneling—Circa 1725

WILTON, HENRICO COUNTY, VA.

Chimney Breast—1732

BROOKE'S BANK, ESSEX COUNTY, VA.

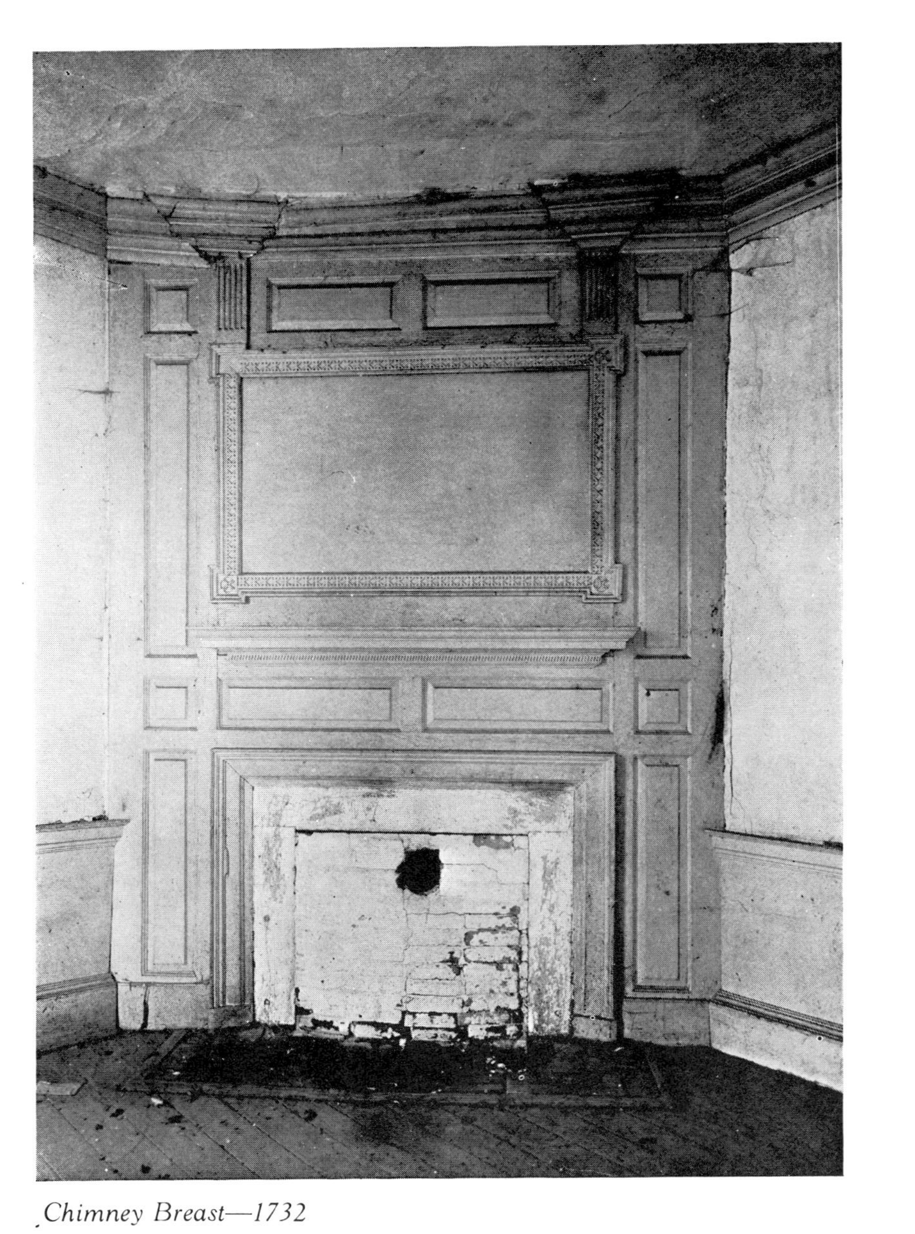

Chimney Breast—1732

BROOKE'S BANK, ESSEX COUNTY, VA.

Chimney Breast—1790

WHITFORD HOUSE, NEW BERN, N. C.

Chimney Breast—1752

CARLYLE HOUSE, ALEXANDRIA, VA.

Chimney Breast—Circa 1726

WESTOVER, CHARLES CITY COUNTY, VA.

Chimney Breast—1752

CARLYLE HOUSE, ALEXANDRIA, VA.

Chimney Breast—1758

MOUNT AIRY, RICHMOND COUNTY, VA.

PLATE 122

Chimney—1770

MENOKIN, RICHMOND COUNTY, VA.

Wedgewood Mantel—1784

MONTICELLO, ALBEMARLE COUNTY, VA.

Chimney Breast—Circa 1790

DONALD HOUSE, NEW BERN, N. C.

Chimney Breast—1790

SMALLWOOD-JONES HOUSE, NEW BERN, N. C.

Chimney Breast and Windows—1790

SMALLWOOD-JONES HOUSE, NEW BERN, N. C.

Mantel—1709

CHELSEA, KING WILLIAM COUNTY, VA.

PLATE 126

Mantel—1725

STRATFORD, WESTMORELAND COUNTY, VA.

Mantel—1725

TUCKAHOE, GOOCHLAND COUNTY, VA.

Mantel (Black Marble)—Circa 1726

WESTOVER, CHARLES CITY COUNTY, VA.

PLATE 128

Mantel Detail—1770

MENOKIN, RICHMOND COUNTY, VA.

Mantel—Circa 1730

LINDSLEY HOUSE, WILLIAMSBURG, VA.

Mantel and Ceiling—1752

KENMORE, FREDERICKSBURG, VA.

Mantel and Cupboard—1755

GUNSTON HALL, FAIRFAX COUNTY, VA.

(Note Gunston Hall Restored 1920)

Mantel—1784

MONTICELLO, ALBEMARLE COUNTY, VA.

Mantel—Circa 1774

ELMWOOD, ESSEX COUNTY, VA.

Mantel—Circa 1793

METROPOLITAN MUSEUM OF ART, NEW YORK

GADSBY'S TAVERN, ALEXANDRIA, VA.

Mantel—Circa 1793

GADSBY'S TAVERN, ALEXANDRIA, VA.

Mantel and Doorways—1658

TODDSBURY, GLOUCESTER COUNTY, VA.

Mantel and Doorways—1726

BERKELEY, CHARLES CITY COUNTY, VA.

PLATE 136

Mantel and Doorways—1658

TODDSBURY, GLOUCESTER COUNTY, VA.

Mantel and Doorways—1730

PEACHY HOUSE, WILLIAMSBURG, VA.

Mantel and Doorway—1751

CARTER'S GROVE, JAMES CITY COUNTY, VA.

(Note Carter's Grove Restored 1929)

Mantel and Doorways—Circa 1730

PEACHY HOUSE, WILLIAMSBURG, VA.

ONE FOOT

ONE FOOT

Transoms and Doorways—Circa 1650

(Note Shirley Restored 1700 and 1770)

SHIRLEY, CHARLES CITY COUNTY, VA.

Doorway—1658
TODDSBURY, GLOUCESTER COUNTY, VA.

Doorway—1650
SHIRLEY, CHARLES CITY COUNTY, VA.
(Restored 1700 and 1770)

Doorway—1658
TODDSBURY, GLOUCESTER COUNTY, VA

Doorway—1668

Doorway—1668

CLAREMONT MANOR, SURRY COUNTY, VA.

(Note Claremont Manor Restored 1929)

Doorway—1698

SHEILD HOUSE, YORKTOWN, VA.

Window—Circa 1658

TODDSBURY, GLOUCESTER COUNTY, VA.

Doorway—Circa 1710

DIGGES HOUSE, YORKTOWN, VA.

Doorway and Paneling—Circa 1710

DIGGES HOUSE, YORKTOWN, VA.

ONE FOOT

Doorway—1730
SCOTCHTOWN, HANOVER COUNTY, VA.

Doorway—1725
TUCKAHOE, GOOCHLAND COUNTY, VA.

Doorway—1784
MONTICELLO, ALBEMARLE COUNTY, VA.

Doorway—Circa 1726

WESTOVER, CHARLES CITY COUNTY, VA.

Doorway—1784

MONTICELLO, ALBEMARLE COUNTY, VA.

Doorway—1752

CARLYLE HOUSE, ALEXANDRIA, VA.

Doorway—1752

KENMORE, FREDERICKSBURG, VA.

Doorway—1755

GUNSTON HALL, FAIRFAX COUNTY, VA.

(Note Gunston Hall Restored 1920)

1709
CHELSEA, KING WILLIAM COUNTY, VA.

Circa 1700
TEMPLE FARM, YORK COUNTY, VA.

1698
SHEILD HOUSE, YORKTOWN, VA.

Window and Ceiling—1752

KENMORE, FREDERICKSBURG, VA.

1755

WYTHE HOUSE
WILLIAMSBURG, VA.

Circa 1700

RITCHIE HOUSE
TAPPAHANNOCK, VA.

1732 Brcoke's

BROOKE'S BANK
ESSEX COUNTY, VA.

1698

SHEILD HOUSE
YORKTOWN, VA.

Windows and Cupboard—Circa 1755

GUNSTON HALL, FAIRFAX COUNTY, VA.

(Note Gunston Hall Restored 1920)

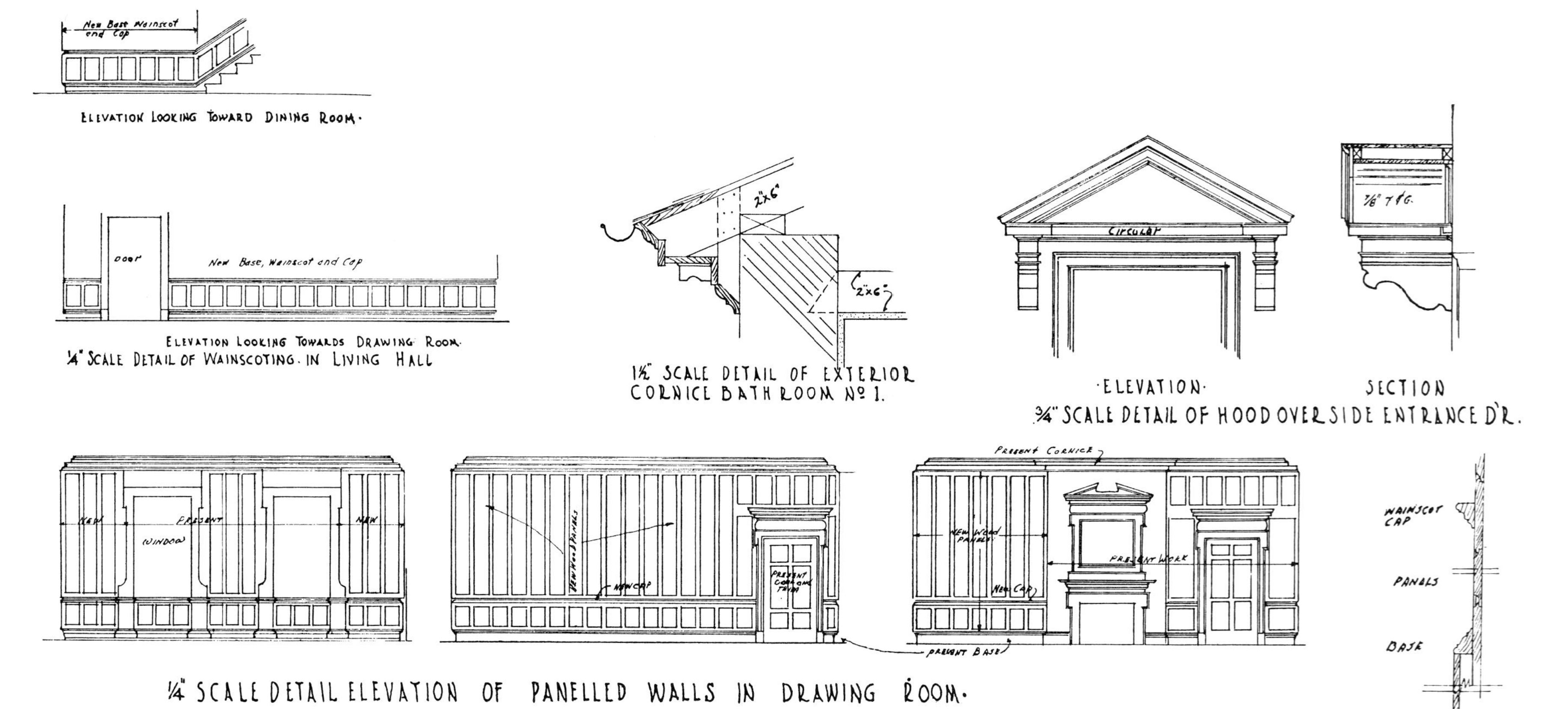
New Base Wainscot and Cap
ELEVATION LOOKING TOWARD DINING ROOM.
Door
New Base, Wainscot and Cap
ELEVATION LOOKING TOWARDS DRAWING ROOM.
1/4" SCALE DETAIL OF WAINSCOTING. IN LIVING HALL
2"x6"
2"x6"
1½" SCALE DETAIL OF EXTERIOR CORNICE BATH ROOM No 1.
Circular
7/8" T&G.
·ELEVATION·
SECTION
3/4" SCALE DETAIL OF HOOD OVER SIDE ENTRANCE D'R.
New
Present
Window
New
New Wood Panels
New Cap
Present Cornice
New Wood Panels
Present Work
New Cap
Present Base
Wainscot Cap
Panels
Base
1½" Scale
1/4" SCALE DETAIL ELEVATION OF PANELLED WALLS IN DRAWING ROOM.

As restored 1927

Drawn by Archie J. Streat

BRANDON, PRINCE GEORGE COUNTY, VA.

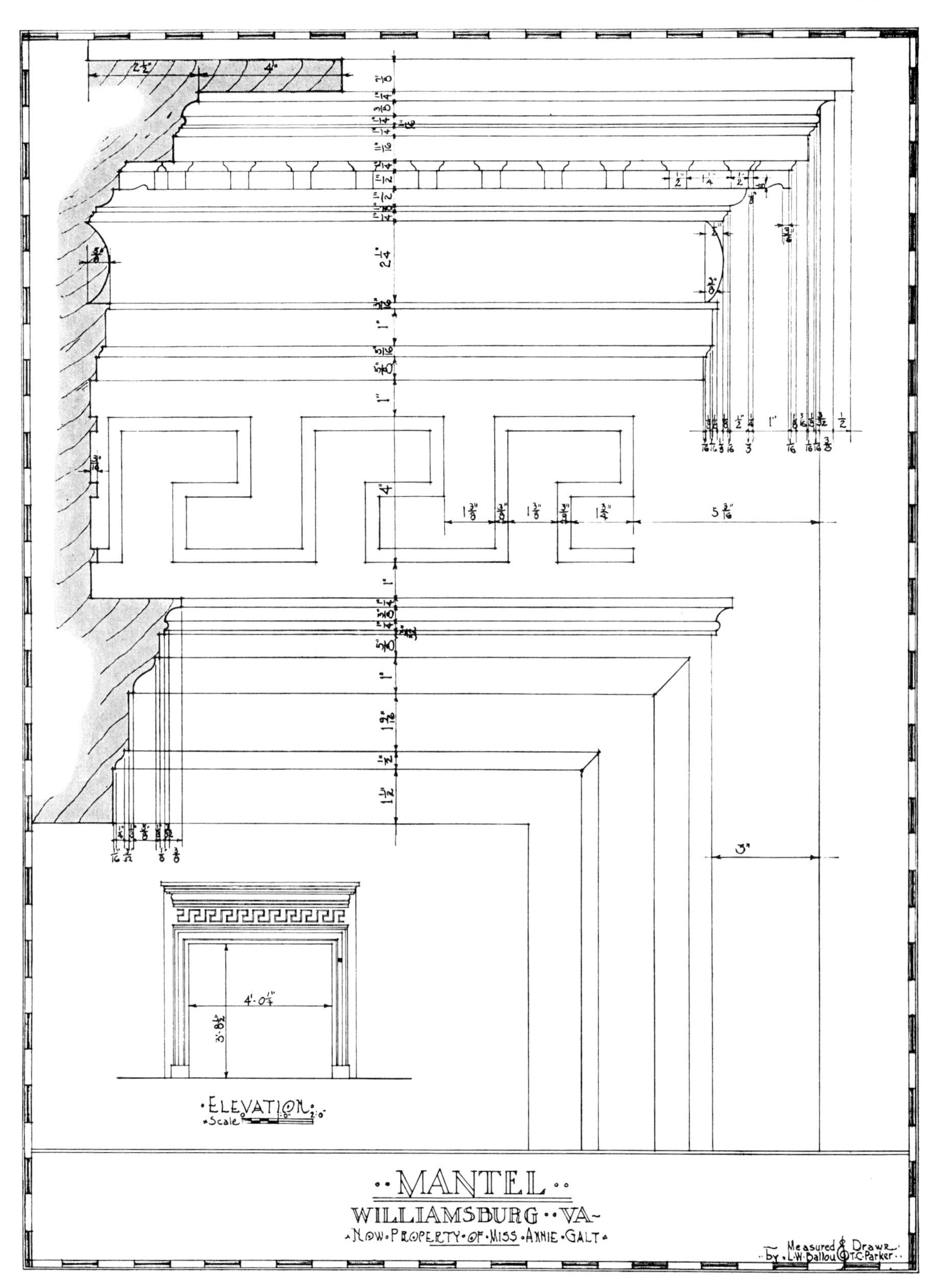
ELEVATION
Scale
MANTEL
WILLIAMSBURG VA
NOW PROPERTY OF MISS ANNIE GALT
Measured & Drawn by L.W. Ballou & T.C. Parker

Measured and drawn by L.W. Ballou and T. C. Parker

LINDSLEY HOUSE, WILLIAMSBURG, VA.

PLATE 154

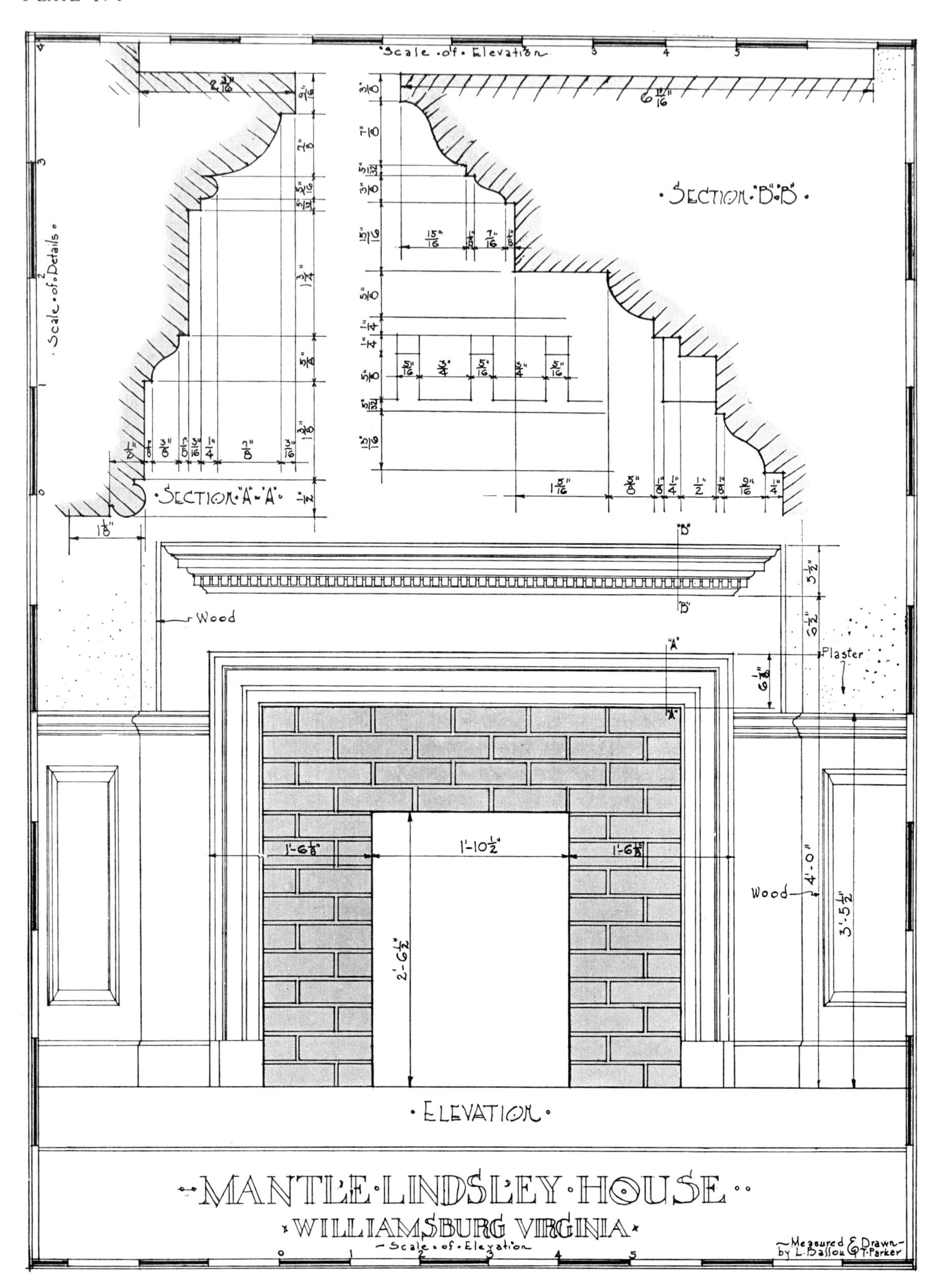
Scale of Elevation
Section "B"-"B"
Section "A"-"A"
Scale of Details
Wood
Plaster
Elevation
MANTLE·LINDSLEY·HOUSE
WILLIAMSBURG VIRGINIA
Scale of Elevation
Measured & Drawn by L. Ballou & T. Parker

Measured and drawn by L. W. Ballou and T. C. Parker

LINDSLEY HOUSE, WILLIAMSBURG, VA.

Ceiling—1752

KENMORE, FREDERICKSBURG, VA.

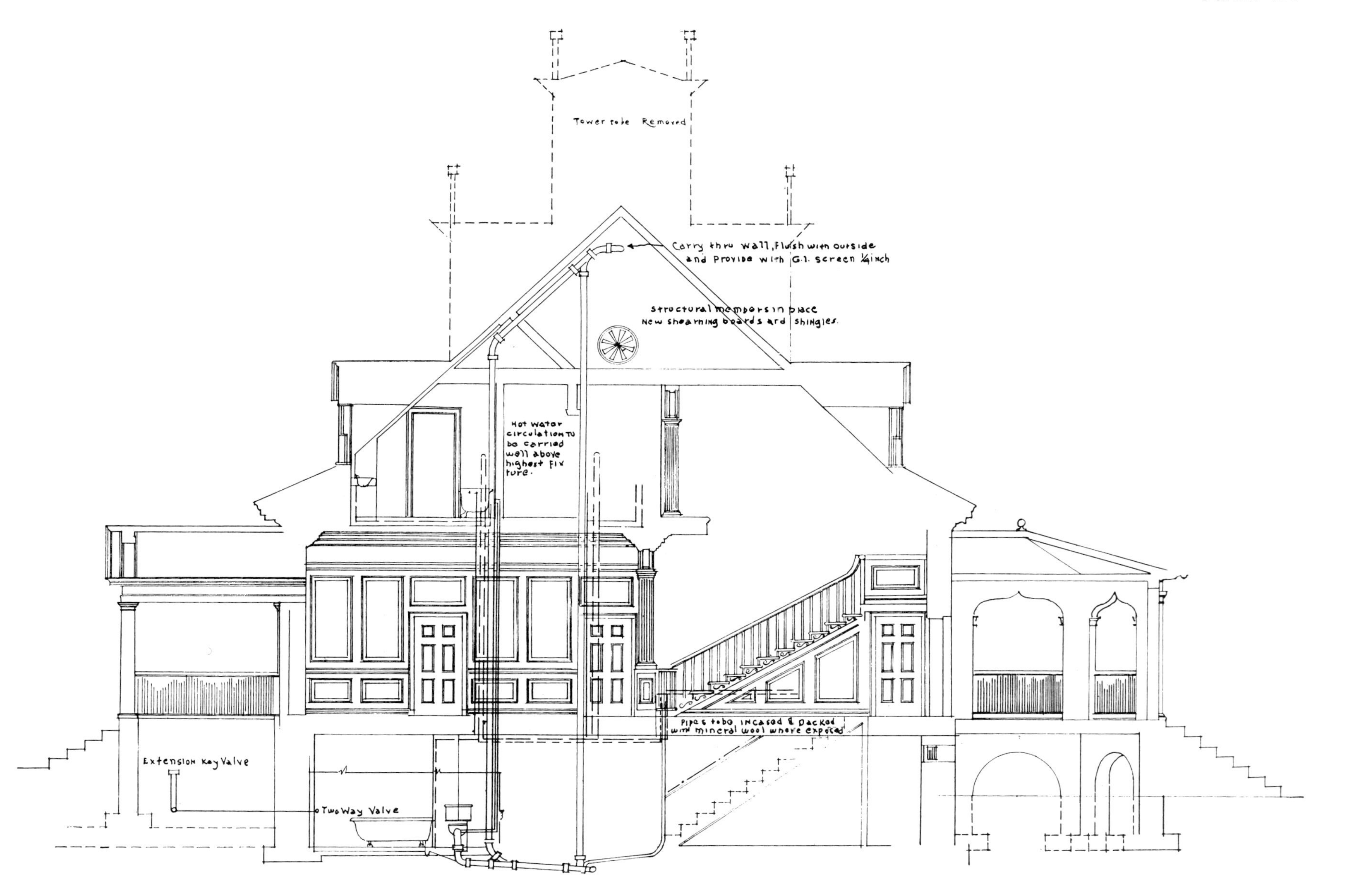

Tower to be Removed
Carry thru wall, Flush with outside and provide with G.I. screen ¼ inch
Structural members in place New sheathing boards and shingles.
Hot water circulation to be carried well above highest fixture.
Pipes to be incased & packed with mineral wool where exposed
Extension Key Valve
Two Way Valve

Cross Section, as restored 1915

Glenn and Bedford Brown, *Architects*

GUNSTON HALL, FAIRFAX COUNTY, VA.

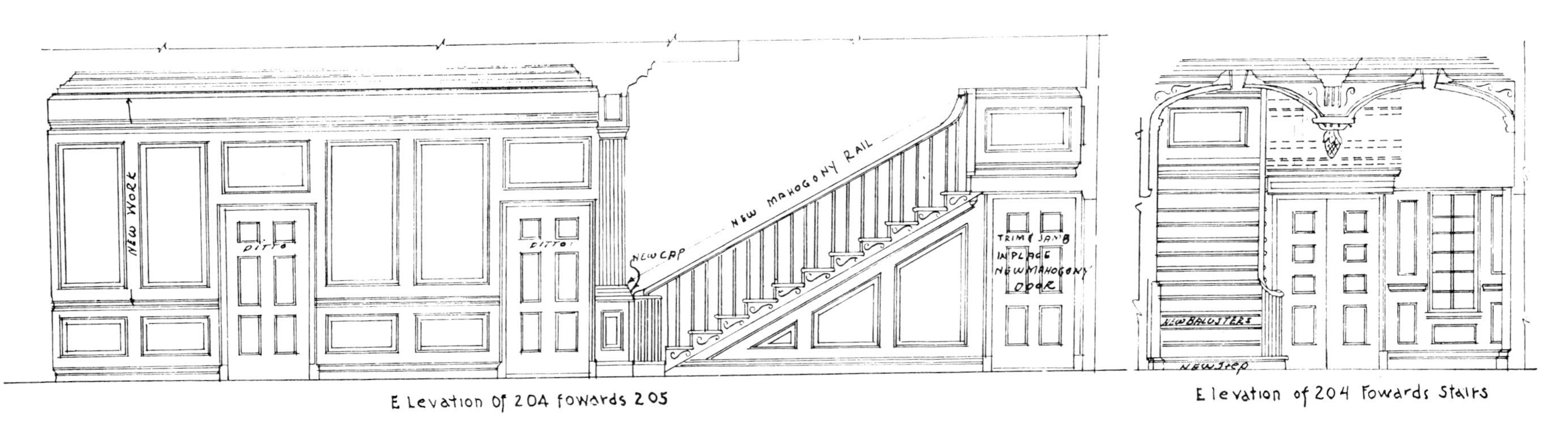
NEW WORK
DITTO
DITTO
NEW CAP
NEW MAHOGONY RAIL
TRIM & JAMB IN PLACE NEW MAHOGONY DOOR
E Levation Of 204 towards 205
NEW BALUSTERS
NEW STEP
E levation of 204 towards Stairs

Stair and Hall Detail

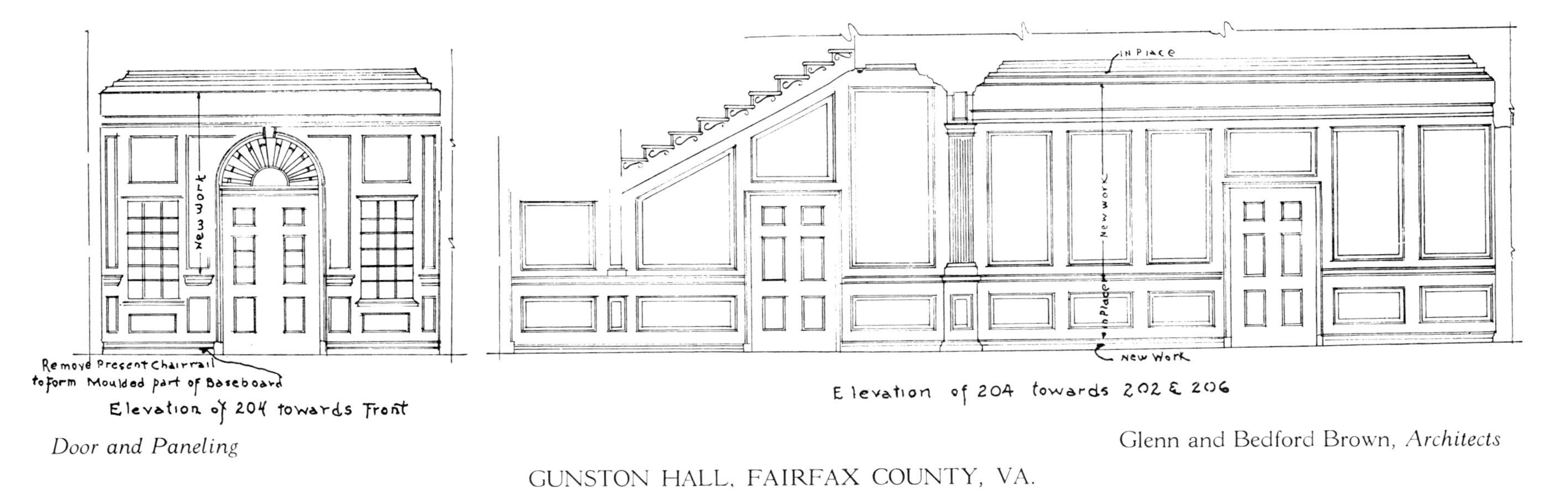
NEW WORK
Remove Present Chairrail to form Moulded part of Baseboard
Elevation of 204 towards Front
IN PLACE
New Work
In Place
New Work
E levation of 204 towards 202 & 206

Door and Paneling

Glenn and Bedford Brown, *Architects*

GUNSTON HALL, FAIRFAX COUNTY, VA.

(Note Gunston Hall Restored 1915)

PLATE 158

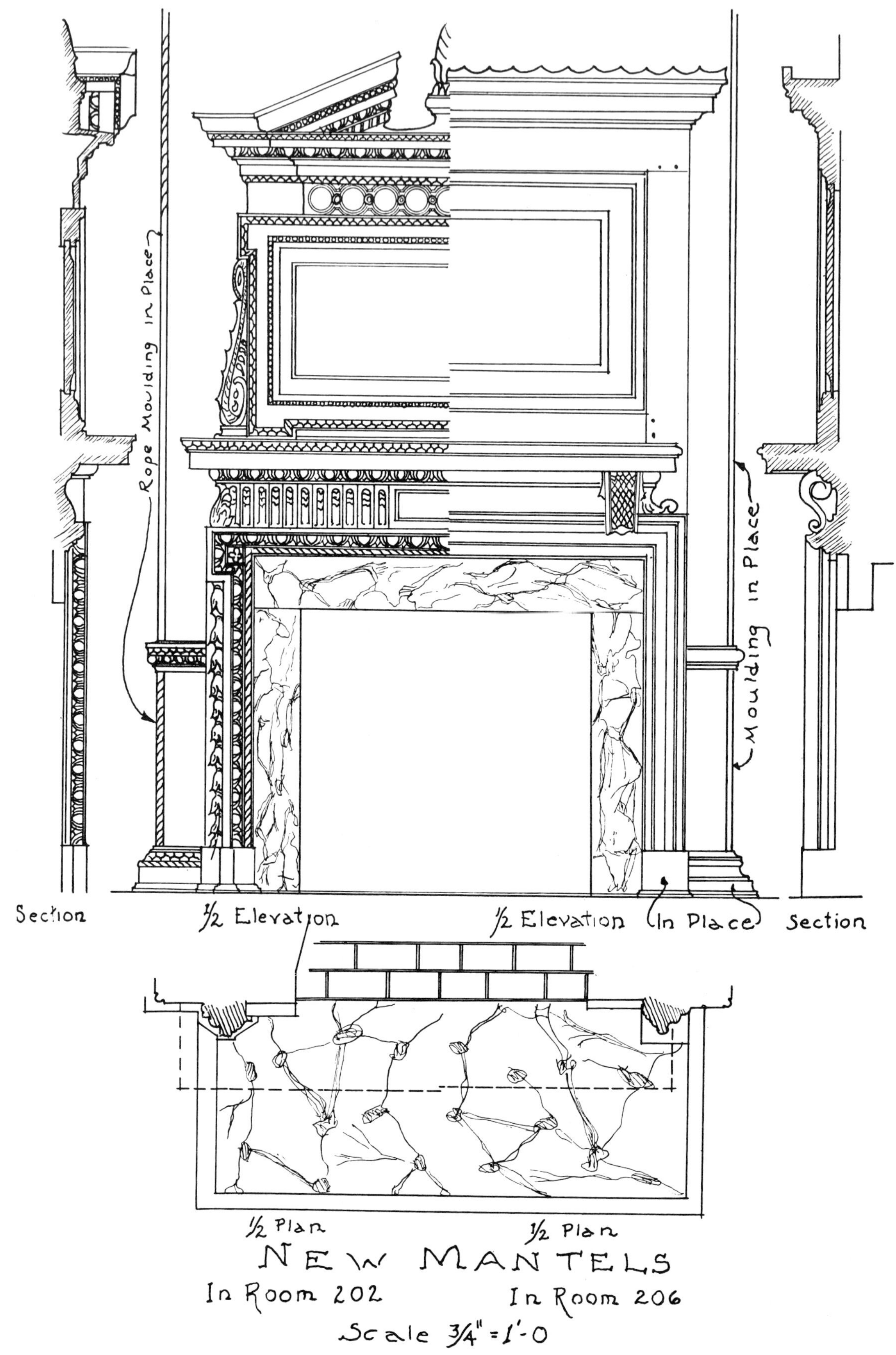
Rope Moulding in Place
Moulding in Place
Section
½ Elevation
½ Elevation
In Place
Section
½ Plan
½ Plan
NEW MANTELS
In Room 202
In Room 206
Scale ¾" = 1'-0

Glenn and Bedford Brown, *Architects*

GUNSTON HALL, FAIRFAX COUNTY, VA.

(Note Gunston Hall Restored 1915)

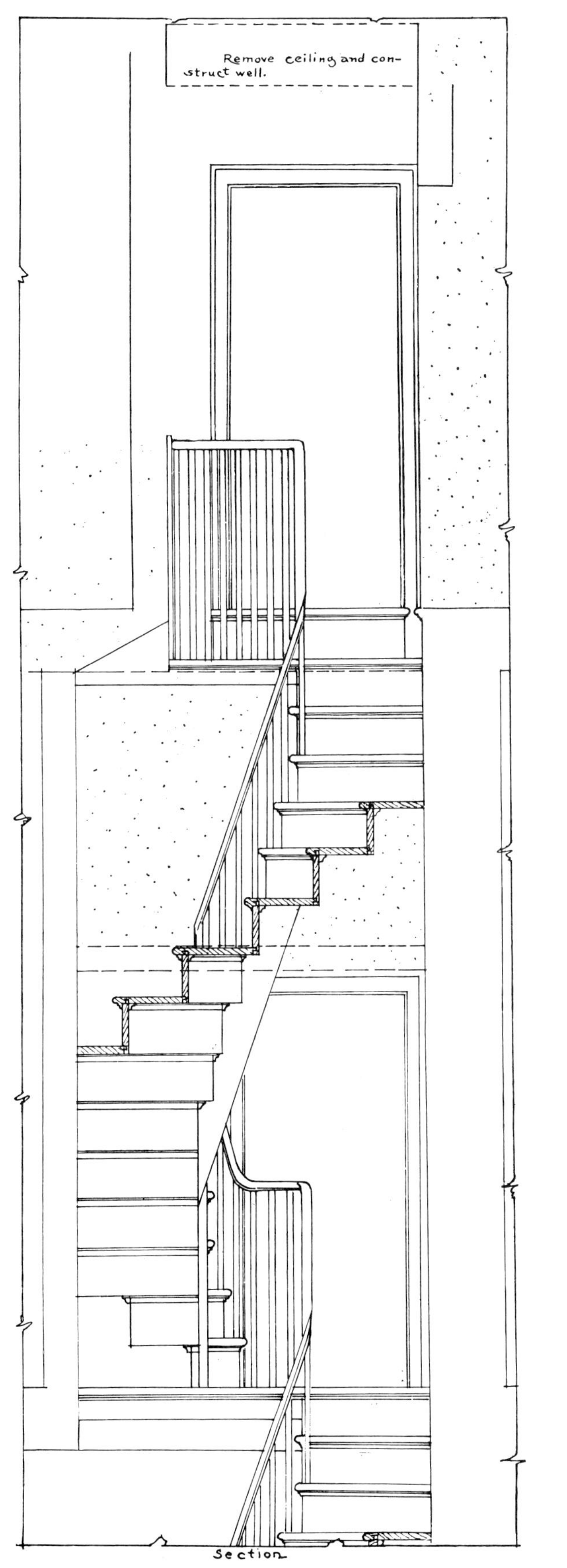
Remove ceiling and construct well.
Section

Rear Stairs Glenn and Bedford Brown, *Architects*

GUNSTON HALL, FAIRFAX COUNTY, VA.

(Note Gunston Hall Restored 1915)